REMARKABLE Women of HARTFORD

CYNTHIA WOLFE BOYNTON

Foreword by GEENA CLONAN
Founding President of Connecticut Women's Hall of Fame

THE
History
PRESS

Published by The History Press
Charleston, SC 29403
www.historypress.net

Back cover, lower: Vintage postcard, year unknown. Danziger & Berman, New Haven, Connecticut.

Unless otherwise noted, images appear courtesy of the author.

First published 2014

ISBN 9781540222879

Library of Congress CIP data applied for.

Notice: The information in this book is true and complete to the best of our knowledge. It is offered without guarantee on the part of the author or The History Press. The author and The History Press disclaim all liability in connection with the use of this book.

*Dedicated to the countless remarkable women I've had the privilege
to know and learn from, most especially my grandmother
Esther Isbel Northrop Wolfe, 1899–1990*

CONTENTS

CONTENTS

FOREWORD

The women featured in this book are truly remarkable. However, also remarkable is the realization that as a field of study, women's history is only in its fourth decade.

The movement to look back while marching forward didn't exist until the 1960s. It was spearheaded by second-wave feminists who, as they worked to advance their own goals and passions, battled pervasive oppression and deep inequalities. When they looked back to discover what they could learn from the lives of their foremothers, they found almost nothing. Traditional history had for the most part ignored outspoken or unpopular women, and few stories and little scholarship existed.

The study of women's history was, in part, established to rectify this and to ensure that no woman or girl would ever again be denied access to the empowerment that stories, historical awareness and effective role models provide. Toward this end, the National Women's Hall of Fame was established in 1969 in the small village of Seneca Falls, New York, where 121 years earlier the fight for equality began with the first Women's Rights Convention. Since then, several states have founded their own women's halls of fame, including Connecticut.

All of the women profiled here in *Remarkable Women of Hartford* have been inducted into the Connecticut Women's Hall of Fame, which can be viewed online at www.cwhf.org. Since its founding in 1994, the Hall has paid well-deserved public tribute to more than one hundred women, honoring their achievements, preserving their legacies and, perhaps even most importantly, educating and inspiring a new generation of women and men alike to follow their beliefs, passions and dreams.

Designed to share these women's struggles and accomplishments, the Hall provides two traveling exhibits, as well as comprehensive educational programs that bring Connecticut women's history to life for both current and future generations. The magnitude of Connecticut Women's Hall of Fame inductees' achievements—as well as the importance of people recognizing and remembering them—can't be stressed enough.

Despite the fact that women make up the majority of our population, their lives and contributions are still overlooked, though much is being done to change this. Congress in 1996 established the nonprofit National Women's History Museum educational center, and fundraising is currently underway to build a permanent museum in Washington, D.C., near the National Mall, that will finally, fully and very visibly integrate women's diverse and significant contributions into our nation's history.

As the Connecticut Women's Hall of Fame and books like *Remarkable Women of Hartford* prove, Connecticut women have been—and continue to be—at the forefront of significant cultural, social, educational, governmental and economic change since America's earliest days. Read on to learn about twelve women whose experiences shaped the lives and practices of those living not only in Hartford or Connecticut but also those living throughout the United States and, in some cases, the world. Their collective stories illustrate the dignity and accomplishments of women from all walks of life and eras. The results of their work are measurable—in fairer public practices, in improved education, in strides toward civil justice, in expanded services for children and families, in greater access to healthcare, in more stable and cooperative communities, and the list goes on. Such is the power of women's history.

GEENA CLONAN
Founding President
Connecticut Women's Hall of Fame

ACKNOWLEDGEMENTS

G reat appreciation and gratitude go to the many people who helped me complete this project, particularly: Adrienne Cochrane, Asha Evans and Andrea Brown Seldon of the Urban League of Greater Hartford; Alyce Perry Englund and the Wadsworth Atheneum; Beth Burgess and Katherine Kane of the Harriet Beecher Stowe Center; Beverly Haynes and Colt Manufacturing; Dennis Barone; Diana McCain and the Connecticut Historical Society; Donna Jolly and Galo Rodriquez at the Village for Children and Families; Geena Clonan and the Connecticut Women's Hall of Fame; Jennifer Sharp and the Hartford Public Library's Hartford History Center; Jim and Susane Grasso; Jodi Mozdzer Gil; Judy Tabar and Planned Parenthood of Connecticut; Linda Smith Cohen and Miriam Butterworth; Linda Glickstein and Rena Koopman; Leslie Fields and the Mount Holyoke College Archives and Special Collections office; Marty Petty, Claude Albert, Joseph Nunes, Jim Smith and the *Hartford Courant*; Maureen Croteau; Patricia Anderson, Maureen Hicks, Lucretia Jackson and Rachel King; Richard, Mallory and Cory Gaines; Rick Standish; and Virginia Hilyard, Ronna Reynolds and The Bushnell Center for the Performing Arts.

Also, special thanks to Carolina Trinidad for ensuring that the images of the women's signatures were as sharp as their original writers; Leslie Cahill at the Graduate Institute for patiently supporting my classic Type 7 behavior; my parents, Barbara and Ted Wolfe, for encouraging my limitless curiosity and making history part of my life; and the three people who try

ACKNOWLEDGEMENTS

their hardest to give me the space and quiet I need to write: my husband, Ted, and sons, Teddy and Steven. Finally, a thank *mew* to Coal the cat, who always knows when a paw on my keyboard will help.

INTRODUCTION

O ne of the many remarkable things I discovered while writing this book was the way these women's lives connected. Virginia Thrall Smith attended the school run by Harriet Beecher Stowe's oldest sister, Catharine. Harriet and her Stowe relatives were known to vacation in Maine with Dotha Bushnell Hillyer. Elizabeth Colt commissioned Lydia Huntley Sigourney to write poems when her husband and children died. Virginia and Ella Grasso both attended Mount Holyoke College. Ella worked with Hilda Crosby Standish and Edythe Gaines. And though a generation separated civil rights activists Mary Townsend Seymour and Rachel Taylor Milton, they both proudly and loudly marched with the NAACP.

Were all these connections coincidences, I wondered? Or were there tangible threads? Certainly geography and timing contributed to some of the women's comings together. For those from older eras, school and work opportunities were limited, so those with similar interests were bound to collide. But it seems that in most instances, the law of human nature also played a part. Like attracts like, and two of the striking characteristics possessed by each of these women were a clear-sighted sense of purpose and a sure belief in her ability to achieve it.

What those purposes were, however, are as different and remarkable as the women themselves. Among them are the medical director of Connecticut's first birth control clinic, Connecticut's first female and African American schools superintendent, the first female U.S. governor elected in her own right and the newswoman who, during the

Revolutionary War, made sure the paper so important to the Patriots' cause never missed an issue.

Those featured here represent a span of more than 230 years of both Hartford and American history. We start with Hannah Bunce Watson, who lived when Connecticut was still a British colony, and end with Ella Grasso and Edythe Gaines, whose staunch beliefs and gender-breaking accomplishments make them leaders of today's Modern Era. In between are those who lived and worked during the mid-1800s Reform Era, in the early twentieth century's Progressive Era and amid two world wars. All of them courageously spoke their minds and sometimes put their lives on the line for the causes they believed in, which included civil justice, women's right to equity, fair business practices, free public schools, healthcare for disabled children and more.

All of these women are role models; their lives are as relevant to life and society today as when they were alive. Yet it's important to note that despite these women's tremendous accomplishments, much of the work they started is still not complete. A century or more since some of their deaths, women and society are still struggling to achieve the wide-reaching freedom, equality and ideals these twelve women so fiercely believed should and could exist.

The number of truly remarkable women who've lived or worked in Hartford made it difficult to choose just those this book could fit. But I'm proud of the cultural, professional and generational diversity represented by those featured here. Others whose lives deserve equal attention and celebration include Isabella Beecher Hooker (Harriet's half sister), 1800s suffragist and leader for improved Connecticut women's property rights; Charlotte Perkins Gilman, author of one of the earliest and most influential works of feminist fiction, "The Yellow Wallpaper"; Edna Negron Rosario, who established the first school-based health clinic in the United States; and Emily Parmely Collins, who dedicated her adult life to women's rights and, in the 1880s, helped found the Hartford Equal Rights Club.

Like the dozen featured on the following pages, they're women whose names might not be as familiar as they once were. Time causes us to forget. And as Harriet Beecher Stowe Center executive director Katherine Kane says in Chapter 3, "Our propensity as people is to look to the future rather than to the past. But looking at the past can help us understand where we are and what we might do to make things better."

This is exactly what I hope this book will do, giving each reader the inspiration needed to be remarkable, too.

CINDY WOLFE BOYNTON

Chapter 1

HANNAH BUNCE WATSON HUDSON

REVOLUTIONARY NEWSPAPER PUBLISHER:
1749–1807

No one knows for sure what inspired twenty-eight-year-old Hannah Bunce Watson to take on the role of publisher of the *Connecticut Courant and Weekly Intelligencer* after her young husband, Ebenezer, died unexpectedly from smallpox in September 1777. Details about her life are as tenuous as the time period in which she lived and inherited the newspaper. As it is today, late 1700s Hartford was the seat of government for the Connecticut Colony. But young America was an unsettled place, having just two months before Ebenezer's death declared itself independent of England and a free state.

Except for the fact that Hannah was born on December 28, 1749, in Lebanon, Connecticut, next to nothing is known about her early years. She and Ebenezer Watson were married in 1770 when Hannah was twenty-one. But by all accounts, she spent no time at the newspaper Ebenezer helped found with Thomas Green and first published on October 29, 1764.

Focused on the home they shared at the south end of Main Street, Hannah was also not involved in her husband's printing business, which, in addition to publishing the weekly *Courant*, produced books, pamphlets, official documents for the Connecticut Colony's General Assembly and fliers supporting the colonies' war against the British.

It's believed that during their seven-year marriage, Hannah spent her days like most colonial women and focused on the "gentle arts"—cooking over an open hearth, spinning wool, sewing, growing kitchen gardens, rendering fat, raising and butchering chickens, attending the ill and rearing children, of

The only known portrait of Hannah, believed to have been drawn in the 1770s. *Hartford Courant.*

which Hannah and Ebenezer had five, the youngest of whom was just seven months old when Ebenezer died at age thirty-four.

But there must have been some kind of fire in Hannah, whether it was sparked by a determination to support her family, a hidden passion for words and writing, a desire to make her own way in the world or something else altogether. Whatever the inspiration, instead of letting the *Courant* and printing house fold after Ebenezer's death, the grieving "Widow Watson" immersed herself in learning the business. She would report, typeset, sell subscriptions and work the presses. She would figure out how to get payments from the many people who owed her husband money, as well as ensure that the *Courant*—at the time the largest newspaper in America's thirteen colonies—continued to report on the Revolutionary War's bloody battles and General George Washington's need for recruits and supplies.

"When I think about Hannah, I think about how gutsy she was," said Marty Petty, the only other woman to serve as publisher of the *Courant*. She held the position from 1997 to 2000, following three years spent as senior vice-president and general manager.

"Men in leadership positions have mentors. They have role models. But women leaders in any time period too often don't have other women to model themselves after," Marty continued. "I didn't have that in Hartford, and Hannah definitely didn't either. I imagine sometimes what a tremendous responsibility she must have felt—the pressure—to get out this newspaper that so many people depended on, and to get it out on time."

Sparked by Fire

In the best of times, Hannah's decision to take over the *Courant* would have no doubt been seen as remarkable. She was grieving, running a household as a single mother and living in a society in which only a handful of women owned property or managed a business or trade. The majority of women lived subservient to men, and those who did find success were too often not taken seriously. However, the fact that, on top of all of this, Hartford and Connecticut were deeply involved in a bloody, draining and often discouraging war makes Hannah's decision astonishing.

British soldiers had destroyed or stopped the presses on newspapers in Boston and other big cities, and only Tory newspapers written by British Loyalists were being published in New York. Delivered by horse to nearby colonies and then distributed by hand, the *Courant* was the only major newspaper at the time printing reports about battles and the Patriot effort. Its existence was vitally important to America's freedom cause, and each issue was an enormous undertaking.

Like most colonial newspapers, the *Courant* consisted of four large pages published once a week. It's believed that at least at the beginning of her tenure as publisher, Hannah was involved in both the editorial and business side, which included not just writing and editing the articles but also selling the advertising needed to offset ink and paper costs and then overseeing the typesetting and printing of each page. It was labor intensive work. After the stories were written and finalized on paper, the person who worked as the composer or typesetter would use blocks of moveable type to construct the words in each article, single letter by letter.

When the page was complete, a pressman would roll ink over the raised words and, with the help of a specially constructed pressurized frame, actually press or imprint them onto a moist sheet of paper. Once dry, he'd then use the same process to hand-print the other side.

"When Hannah became publisher, she followed a route that was unfamiliar but not unpaved by widows with children to support," said University of Connecticut journalism professor and department head Maureen Croteau, noting that at various times throughout the 1700s, women edited roughly sixteen of the seventy-eight small newspapers that circulated in the colonies. Among the most well-known presswomen were Elizabeth Timothy, a 1730s printer and newspaper publisher in South Carolina who worked for Benjamin Franklin, and Elizabeth Glover of Massachusetts, who, after her husband died in 1638, founded the first printing press in the colonies, the Cambridge Press.

Hannah oversaw the publication of roughly sixty issues of the *Connecticut Courant*, including this one from December 1777. *Connecticut Historical Society.*

"Although printing and newspaper publishing were definitely regarded as men's jobs, a woman in Watson's position had few good alternatives. Economic survival centered around marriage. Preserving the family business, at least long enough for a son or a new husband to take over, was often the only course," Croteau continued. "It's difficult today to fully appreciate the strength of such women. Proficient at the gentle arts, they were deemed unsuited to the challenges of the business world. Watson proved how faulty that reasoning was."

It's unclear what caused Hannah to eventually decide that juggling multiple responsibilities was more than she could or wanted to handle. Hannah left no known diaries or letters. What is clear, however, is that by January 1778, she recognized the need for a partner, which she found in *Courant* composer and printer George Goodwin. At twenty, George was already an experienced pressman, having been hired by Ebenezer when he was just nine years old.

With George responsible for the production end of the newspaper, Hannah could focus on the business end, which included seeking out past-due payments totaling more than £2,400 (roughly $3,800 by today's conversion rates and a small fortune in colonial times) from about two hundred subscribers, advertisers and other printing clients. And apparently, she was not shy about asking, as this notice she published in the *Courant* well illustrates:

> [If the *Connecticut Courant* failed,] *the public will view it as an inevitable misfortune in which they are called to share. Under the circumstances, it is scarcely necessary to mention that HUMANITY, as well as JUSTICE, obliges every one who is indebted to the estate of Mr. WATSON, deceas'd, to make immediate payment.*

Battling the Blaze

If this new partnership with George Goodwin caused Hannah to experience any feelings of relief, they didn't last long. Just three weeks later on January 27, 1778, the paper mill that provided all the *Courant's* newsprint and that Hannah co-owned with fellow widow Sarah Ledyard "burnt to ashes." At the time, most believed the fire was set by prisoners of war or Tories—British Loyalists looking to shut down the last remaining Patriot newspaper by destroying its paper supply.

And indeed, the blaze was devastating. With so many of Ebenezer's debts still unpaid, the *Courant* had no money to buy replacement paper, let alone rebuild the mill. For the newspaper to continue, it would need not just hundreds of reams of printing paper but also all new printing equipment to replace what was now ash. Seeing no other option, Hannah and George announced that the *Courant* had no choice but fold.

Yet as many recognized, the paper was more than a business. It was an essential tool in the Patriot cause. Without the *Courant*, there was no reliable, widespread way to disperse the word about America's battlefield victories or request the supplies desperately needed to support the freezing, hungry and cramped soldiers encamped with Washington, Lafayette and the other Revolutionary leaders in Valley Forge, Pennsylvania.

Four other smaller Connecticut newspapers also got their paper from the mill, and Hannah and Sarah's realization of its importance sparked an idea. Stressing how much the Continental army relied on the *Courant* and the mill, the two women appealed to the Connecticut General Assembly for permission to hold a fundraising lottery. Legislators responded immediately,

PAPER-MILL
LOTTERY.

GRANTED by the GENERAL ASSEMBLY of the
State of CONNECTICUT January 1778. to raise
the Sum of Fifteen Hundred Pounds for the Benefit of
Mrs. SARAH LEDYARD and Mrs. HANNAH WATSON
Widows, who were the Owners of the Paper-Mill in
Hartford lately consumed by fire. and to enable them
to rebuild the same they having given Bond to the
Treasurer of the State to appropriate the Money ac-
cording to Resolution of said Assembly.

S C H E M E.

6000 Tickets at 6 Dollars each is   36000 Dollars.
Deduct for the Use of the Paper-Mill   5000 Do.
                                       ─────
To be drawn in Prizes as below   31000 Do.

1 Prize of	2500 Dollars is	1500 Dollars.
1 Do	800 Do	800 Do.
2 Do	400 Do	800 Do.
4 Do	200 Do	800 Do.
10 Do	100 Do	1000 Do
20 Do	50 Do	1000 Do.
30 Do	30 Do	900 Do.
100 Do	20 Do	2000 Do.
1850 Do	12 Do	22200 Do.
2018 Prizes		31000 Dollars.

To raise the $5,000 needed to rebuild the
Courant's paper mill, Hannah and her mill co-
owner conducted a lottery—an unorthodox and
revolutionary idea for the time. *Hartford Courant.*

approving the plan and noting the "public necessity and utility" of the mill.

Hartford residents Dr. Solomon Smith, Samuel Talcott Jr. and James Bill were appointed to manage the lottery, which would consist of six thousand tickets sold at approximately $6 each. This would raise the £1,500, or $5,000, needed to rebuild the mill. The remaining $31,000 would be paid out in prizes to the winners.

Clearly, the idea was well received. Within two weeks, lottery managers said ticket sales had "exceeded their most sanguine expectations," and two weeks later, tickets were sold out. Advertisements for carpenters to rebuild the mill began running in the *Courant*, which Hannah had managed to continue publishing on odd sizes and stocks of paper. Editions varied in length and shape and often were just two pages rather than the *Courant's* usual four. Some editions were even published on wrapping paper, but the paper never missed an issue. Today, thanks in big part to Hannah's clever mind and determination, the daily *Hartford Courant* is able to truthfully call itself the oldest continually published newspaper in the nation.

The mill was rebuilt by the spring of 1778. And as summer rolled in, topping the *Courant's* pages above short articles about lost steers, temperance meetings and church services were letters from the troops at Valley Forge. Many issues included reports written by General Washington himself, including a long, detailed account of the Battle of Monmouth Courthouse in New Jersey, where ten thousand Americans fought the same number of British soldiers to a draw.

Under Hannah's leadership, the *Courant* kept a close eye on the war, as well as offered pointed commentary. "THE BRITISH PHARAOH'S SPEECH TO

His Venal Parliment" was how the *Courant* described one of King George III's addresses justifying the war. Other articles criticized war profiteering, advocated for higher taxes in the colonies to pay for soldiers' salaries and encouraged colonists to make "the greatest exertions" needed to donate the clothing, supplies and money the Patriot army needed. The frequency of patriotic poems that appeared suggests Hannah had a love of verse:

> *But Britain, oh! how painful 'til to tell!*
> *Commits a sin that makes it blush in hell.*

Bogged down with the day-to-day businesses of running the Connecticut Colony's largest newspaper and still behind on collecting money from those who owed her late husband, Hannah turned to her next-door neighbor Barzillai Hudson, a successful businessman who years earlier had worked for Ebenezer as a bill collector. Recently widowed, thirty-seven-year-old Barzillai stepped in to help, and several months later on February 11, 1779, he and Hannah were married. Like so much about Hannah, it's not known whether she married Barzillai for love, comfort, convenience, a mix of these or for other reasons altogether. But shortly after becoming Hannah Hudson, she turned over all her possessions and property to him as was required by law—including the *Courant.*

Seventeen months after becoming the first female publisher of the *Connecticut Courant,* Hannah stepped back and watched as Watson & Goodwin dissolved and Hudson & Goodwin formed. Barzillai assumed the role of the *Courant*'s publisher and senior editor, and Hannah turned her attention to home, which was now filled with her and Barzillai's combined seven children.

Together, Hannah and Barzillai went on to have another son and three daughters, bringing their brood to a whopping eleven. Their son Henry grew up to become mayor of Hartford, serving from 1836 to 1840. By then, Hartford was no longer the colony of 2,500 people that Hannah, through her role as *Courant* publisher, had helped shape but a city of more than 10,000. In 1837, her weekly *Courant* also became a daily.

Hannah, unfortunately, was not there to see her son, hometown or newspaper thrive. She died on September 26, 1807 at just fifty-eight years old and without her husband by her side. While she lay ill, Barzillai and George Goodwin were on trial before the U.S. Supreme Court for criminal libel after publishing a story that alleged President Thomas Jefferson had attempted to use tons of silver to bribe French leader Napoleon Bonaparte to stop seizing U.S. ships.

DIED—In this city, on Sunday last, Mrs. HANNAH HUDSON, wife of Mr. Barzillai Hudson, senior editor of this paper, aged 58 years.

Just a few short lines in the September 30, 1807 *Connecticut Courant* marked the death of the woman responsible for the paper's survival. *Hartford Courant.*

Hannah's worn and partially sunken grave at Hartford's Old South Burying Ground on Maple Avenue.

Her tiny, almost unnoticeable obituary was buried in the *Courant* between two longer news briefs—the one above announcing the marriage of Miss Mary Hall of Hartford to Mr. Ray May of Savannah and the one below explaining how a woman named Elizabeth Hitchcock died after a four-month illness and just a few weeks shy of her 101st birthday. Hannah's death notice read, "Died—In this city, on Sunday last, Mrs. Hannah Hudson, wife of Barzillai Hudson, senior editor of this newspaper, aged 58 years."

Hannah Bunce Watson Hudson is buried next to Barzillai in a far corner of Hartford's Old South Burying Ground at 400 Maple Avenue. An urn and willow—popular motifs in the nineteenth century—are carved into the top of her tall brownstone headstone, which is spotted with mold and has begun to sink into the ground. It's a forgotten place. One of the oldest cemeteries in the city, the grass is too tall, litter lines the fence, many of the stones surrounding Hannah's are broken and few of the graves show signs of any recent visitors.

"Hannah is the matriarch of the *Hartford Courant*," Marty Petty said. "She deserves to be remembered for what she did to keep the paper running after the fire but also for being a strong woman. We don't know a lot about her, but some things are clear, like the fact she was a risk taker and someone willing to push on through adversity to find a way to get things done."

In other words, Hannah was remarkable, a revolutionary woman in a revolutionary time.

Chapter 2

LYDIA HUNTLEY SIGOURNEY

INDEPENDENT FEMALE WRITER: 1791–1865

Lydia Huntley Sigourney believed that when women spoke, their words needed to do three things:

1. Give pleasure.
2. Be instructive.
3. Provide comfort.

In her 1833 advice book *Letters to Young Ladies*, Sigourney also extolled the virtues of women who read aloud, wrote lively letters and never "permitted the mind to slumber at its post." Rather, it was a woman's responsibility to find and use her talents. She wrote, "Our individual privileges, as well as the energetic character of the age, demand persevering exertions. We are enriched with gifts to which our ancestors were strangers. Our responsibilities are proportionally greater…By the shortness of life, we are also admonished to perpetual industry."

Undoubtedly, Lydia Huntley Sigourney was reflecting on her own work habits and commitments when she wrote this passage, the last line especially. One of the first women in America to financially support herself and her family as a writer, Lydia was among the most popular and prolific authors of the nineteenth century. Despite that fact that women in this era were not encouraged to obtain an education or pursue a professional career (instead expected to focus on home and family), Lydia published close to sixty books in her lifetime that ranged from memoirs to travelogues to poetry collections. It's a body of work that, in retrospect, even the 1800s male writers who dismissed her as a "scribbling woman"—Mark Twain and Nathaniel

Early portrait from Lydia's 1866 autobiography, *Letters of Life*. *Harriet Beecher Stowe Center, Hartford, Connecticut.*

Hawthorne among them—would have to acknowledge as impressive. By the time of her death in June 1865, she was so beloved in Hartford that on the day of her funeral, church bells throughout the city rang for an hour.

"Profit-wise, she may be the most successful writer of her time, and content-wise too," said Saint Joseph College American Studies program director Dennis Barone. An English professor and poet laureate for the city of West Hartford, his most recent book, *Garnet Poems: An Anthology of Connecticut Poetry Since 1776,* includes a section on Lydia.

"She didn't just write in one genre, she wrote in several—advice books, history books, meditations—though she's best known for her poetry," Barone continued. "Many of her books like *Letters to Young Ladies* were so popular that they went back to print many times. But Twain, Hawthorne, [Edgar Allan] Poe and other popular male writers from the time eventually overshadowed her, and she and her words faded out."

Synonymous with a City

It's impossible to travel through Hartford and not see the name "Sigourney" (pronounced *Sig-ER-knee*). Interstates 91 and 84 both exit onto the mile-long Sigourney Street, plus there's a Sigourney parking garage, housing complex, market and almost three-acre city park. All are named after Lydia, whose simply worded, straightforward prose and poetry focused on moral issues like slavery, current events like the western movement sparked by the laying of the transcontinental railroad and common experiences like death. Death, in fact, was one of Lydia's

Lydia's signature, 1861. *Harriet Beecher Stowe Center, Hartford, Connecticut.*

favorite subjects. She wrote about it at length and in several forms, often focusing on the death of children, such as she did in "Death of an Infant":

> *Death found strange beauty on that cherub brow,*
> *And dash'd it out. There was a tint of rose*
> *On cheek and lip;—he touch'd the veins with ice,*
> *And the rose faded.—Forth from those blue eyes*
> *There spoke a wishful tenderness,—a doubt*
> *Whether to grieve or sleep, which Innocence*
> *Alone can wear. With ruthless haste he bound*
> *The silken fringes of the curtaining lids*
> *For ever. There had been a murmuring sound*
> *With which the babe would claim its mother's ear,*
> *Charming her even to tears. The spoiler set*
> *His seal of silence. But there beam'd a smile*
> *So fix'd and holy from that marble brow,—*
> *Death gazed and left it there;—he dared not steal*
> *The signet-ring of Heaven.*

The idea that death was an escape to a better place was a common theme in Victorian literature, and Lydia was often commissioned to write poems or elegies for deceased friends and acquaintances. Traditional gender roles—the "separate spheres" that women's rights activists at the time were working so hard to dismiss—were another of Lydia's favorite themes. Many of her works talked about responsibility and religion as well as drew on images from the Bible, encouraging readers to be compassionate, believe in God and embrace all races and faces. Many church choirs sung her religious poems as hymns.

Some of her most popular works tackled what she believed were injustices being done to the poor, oppressed and underserved. Farmers, slaves and especially Native Americans were too often mistreated, Lydia believed, and their plights too often forgotten. It's a topic she tackled most famously in the poem "Indian Names":

> *Ye say they all have passed away,*
> *That noble race and brave,*
> *That their light canoes have vanished*
> *From off the crested wave;*
> *That 'mid the forests where they roamed*
> *There rings no hunter shout,*
> *But their name is on your waters,*
> *Ye may not wash it out.*

Continuing on for several more stanzas, the poem also alludes to the spirits Lydia believed lived in nature as well as shows the inextricable connection she saw between people and place. If a poet today were to write a similar poem about Lydia, the setting would undoubtedly be Hartford, where like the Native Americans in Lydia's "Indian Names," her "everlasting rivers speak."

Born on September 1, 1791, in Norwich, Connecticut, Lydia Howard Huntley was the only child of Zerviah Wentworth and Ezekiel Huntley. Her father, who fought in the Civil War, was a gardener and man known for his "stainless integrity and amiable piety," said an article in the September 1, 1858 *Cosmopolitan Art Journal*. Her mother, the *Journal* continued, was quick, perceptive and sensible, while Lydia was an obedient child who, the article claimed, read her first book at three and wrote her first poem at seven. Most historians say she wrote her first poem at age thirteen to honor the death of the woman her father worked for.

Bright and curious, she attended girls schools in Norwich and Hartford and, after she graduated, opened her own. Her first school in Norwich closed fairly quickly, after Lydia's partner became too ill to teach. Lydia then opened a second in Hartford, which for five years held classes in the home of acquaintance Daniel Wadsworth, a wealthy artist and architect who in 1842 founded Hartford's Wadsworth Atheneum. Lydia's students were Daniel's friends' daughters, whom she greatly impacted, said an article that ran two days after Lydia's death in the June 12, 1865 *Hartford Courant:* "Many of the mothers of the present day had the advantage of her instructions, and cherish the deepest gratitude for her teachings and her example."

In 1815, Daniel Wadsworth also helped Lydia publish her first book, *Moral Pieces in Prose and Verse.*

Neither the mansion Lydia and her husband, Charles, lived in at 15 Hurlburt Street nor the street itself exist in Hartford today. *Library of Congress.*

In her autobiography, *Letters of Life,* which was published a year after she died, Lydia described the decision she made in her twenties to never marry so she would always be available to care for her parents and give back "the absorbing love" that even "the longest life-service" could not repay:

> *My mind was made up never to leave my parents…I had seen aged people surrounded by indifferent persons, who considered their care a burden, and could not endure the thought that my tender parents, who were without near relatives, should be thrown upon the fluctuating kindness of hirelings and strangers. To me, my father already seemed aged, though scarcely sixty; and I said, in my musing hours, "Shall he, who never denied me aught, or spoke to me otherwise than in love-tones, stretch forth his hands in their weakness, and find none to gird him?"*

A suitor soon did win her heart, however: prominent Hartford widower and businessman Charles Sigourney, who Lydia met through Daniel. Following convention at the time, Lydia gave up the school when she married Charles in 1819. A traditionalist, he also wanted her to stop writing, except for when she had "leisure time." Apparently, "public authorship" was not something to be proud of, Charles thought, though Lydia did not agree. She would indeed write. Their compromise was that she would publish her books, essays and poems anonymously, which is why in early editions of *Letters to Young Ladies* and a second advice book called *How to Be Happy*, the author is simply listed as "By a Lady." Similarly, her story "The Farmer and the Soldier" was printed under the name L.H.S. and several works simply as by Anonymous.

But Lydia's work was enormously popular. It sold well, earning Lydia an income, which proved to be much needed when Charles's business began to sink. At roughly the same time, word began to spread that she was the author of the much sought-after *Letters to Young Ladies*, which by that time was going into its twenty-fifth printing. Her identity known, Lydia began publishing under her own name, and the volume of work she produced that first year after was truly remarkable. In just twelve months, she wrote not just several newspaper and magazine articles but also nine books, including a biography, a history book and a poetry collection. Truly, she was practicing the words she preached, living each day in the state of "perpetual industry" that she saw so essential to womanhood.

Yet she also had skills in the "realm of men" and, in addition to writing, became known among publishers for her savvy to negotiate contracts and maneuver substantial royalties for her works. Her name also drew enough attention that for several years, editors of the monthly *Godey's Lady's Book* paid her an at-the-time unheard of $500 annual salary to include her name in the magazine's masthead.

This hefty, steady income allowed her to comfortably contribute to her and Charles's household, support her ailing parents and give as much as 10 percent of her earnings to charity. It also gave her the opportunity to spend a year living, writing and speaking in England and France. There, according to the June 1865 *Hartford Courant*, "Her reputation had preceded her, and she was received in the highest literary circles of both countries, as well as in the most select private society with the profoundest respect, and the most flattering attentions."

Yet critics, especially Twain, continued to dismiss her work. A fellow Hartford resident, Twain went as far as to parody Lydia in a scene in *The Adventures of Huckleberry Finn*. Those who know Twain's novel will find it in the chapter in which Huck finds shelter with a family after a steamboat destroys his and Jim's raft. Around the family's house are grim cemetery paintings of a deceased daughter, Emmeline, and in a scrapbook a death poem that Emmeline wrote:

And did young Stephen sicken,
And did young Stephen die?
And did the sad hearts thicken,
And did the mourners cry?

"She warn't particular," the family tells Huck. "She could write about anything you choose to give her to write about, just so it was sadful. Every time a man died, or a woman died, or a child died, she would be on hand with her 'tribute' before he was cold."

As cruel as it was, in fairness to Twain, he wasn't the only one who grimaced at Lydia's tendency to muse on death. "Her muse of inspiration bore more resemblance to the grim reaper than to an ethereal will-o'-the-wisp," a teacher at Miss Porter's School in Farmington told the *Hartford Courant* in 1985 in response to a collection of Lydia's papers being donated to the Hartford Public Library.

A Legacy of Words

Known as "the sweet singer of Hartford," Lydia Huntley Sigourney was unarguably one of the most popular writers of her day. Sadly, today, her work is mostly forgotten, although among academics, there's been something of a resurgence of interest. But for most in the general public, the name Sigourney is most associated with a downtown Hartford street.

"It's a shame, because so many of the issues she wrote about are very relevant today," added Saint Joseph College's Professor Barone. "Poverty, civil justice, oppression, education are all issues Lydia explored in her work and very much relate to the present. It would be wonderful if there could be a renewed interest in this remarkable woman and her writing. One hundred years ago, she inspired many young women to become poets."

During the nineteenth century, she was also one of the inspirations of the lyceum movement—most simply defined as one of the earliest forms of adult education—in which lecturers, authors, entertainers and scholars would travel around the country from venue to venue, speaking, debating and entertaining. Many of these events were held at meetings hosted by a particular group or society. Lydia's writing, particularly her advice and self-help writing that encouraged women to discover their best and fullest lives, led to the establishment of dozens of literary societies and study clubs.

Lydia in the last decade of her life. *Brady-Handy Photograph Collection, Library of Congress.*

Lydia's grave at Spring Grove Cemetery in Hartford. It's located in the center section, under an elm tree.

Consisting primarily of women, groups with names like the Sigourney Society, Sigourney Literary Society, Young Ladies' Sigournean Band and Sigournean Club formed in places as diverse as Oxford, New York; Gaffney, South Carolina; Centerville, Indiana; Batavia, Illinois; and Winfield, Kansas.

And Lydia appreciated her readers as much as they appreciated her. Especially in her later years, she was known to pay for the publishing of some of her books so she could give away copies for free. She also reported in her autobiography that during an average year, she responded to as many as two thousand letters, many of which included requests for specially written poems, including one that asked that she write an elegy to a dead canary.

A few years before Lydia's death in 1865, residents of Keokuk County, Iowa, renamed their county seat Sigourney. According to the 2010 U.S. census, 2,059 people currently live in Sigourney, Iowa, a city that bills itself as a place "Where tradition meets tomorrow." Its name can be credited to 1800s county commissioner Dr. George Stone, who clearly was an ardent admirer of Lydia's work. Characteristically humble, Lydia was so flattered by the recognition that she gave the town several trees, which officials planted in the courtyard near its courthouse. A large oil painting of Lydia also hangs in the Sigourney courthouse foyer.

When she died, the *Hartford Courant* offered a retrospective of her life, observing:

> *Her first productions were remarkable for the purity and severe simplicity of their style. Turning back to these now, we find in their abstinence from excessive ornament, and in their evident reserved power, little to remind us*

that they are the productions of a young person under twenty years of age. As she advanced in strength of mind and power of expression, the same self-imposed restraint was continued. She had every temptation to indulge in the besetting sin, then as well as now, of American writers—extravagance of thought and expression—for she had the perfect control of a rich and copious diction, and her fancy and imagination were so fertile and creative, that she had only to remove the restraint placed upon them by the accuracy of her judgment, and the severity of her taste, and her flight would have been in the mid-heavens...Her merit, in our judgment, greatly consists in the rigid restraint with which she curbed herself, the national tendency to redundancy and inflation of style, giving us in her writings, prose as well as verse, models of pure and elegant English.

Quaker poet and abolitionist John Greenleaf Whittier paid tribute to his friend this way:

She sang alone, ere womanhood had known
The gift of song which fills the air to-day:
Tender and sweet, a music all her own
May fitly linger where she knelt to pray.

Since her death, several respected literary publishers and scholars like Barone have included Lydia's poems and other works in anthologies. Thanks to the Poetry Foundation, the nonprofit Internet Archive and similar organizations, many of Lydia's works—including full-length books—can also be found online and read and downloaded for free. Among them is *Letters of Life*, in which Lydia looked back on her career, writing, "My literary course has been a happy one. It commenced in impulse, and was continued from habit. Two principles it has ever kept in view—not to interfere with the discharge of womanly duty, and to aim at being an instrument of good."

More people should share Lydia's remarkable path.

Chapter 3

HARRIET BEECHER STOWE

COURAGEOUS ABOLITIONIST AND AUTHOR:
1811–1896

*I wrote what I did because as a woman, as a mother, I was oppressed
and broken-hearted with the sorrows and injustice I saw, because as a
Christian I felt the dishonor to Christianity—because as a lover of my
county, I trembled at the coming day of wrath.*

These words are proof that no one can tell Harriet Beecher Stowe's remarkable
story more powerfully than Harriet herself, who, when she died at the age
of eighty-five on July 1, 1896, was eulogized as one of the most influential writers
of the nineteenth century. A passionate abolitionist, her best-known novel, *Uncle
Tom's Cabin*, had such a wide and powerful impact on Americans' feelings about
slavery that legend says a year into the Civil War, President Abraham Lincoln
credited her as "the little lady who started this big war."

Harriet, however, was the author of more than just this one book, as well
as more than just an author and abolitionist. The daughter of a Presbyterian
minister, she was also a passionate women's rights activist, religion reformer,
equal education advocate and, later in life, a spiritualist who held séances,
believing that with an open mind and the help of mediums, the living could
talk to the dead. She was also a woman who believed she could make a
difference and, perhaps through her words and actions, inspire others to
make a difference too. According to her, "When you get into a tight place
and everything goes against you until it seems that you cannot hold on for
a minute longer, never give up then, for that is just the place and time when
the tide will turn."

Harriet seated in the parlor of her Forest Street home, August 1886. *Harriet Beecher Stowe Center, Hartford, Connecticut.*

A Step into History

At the Harriet Beecher Stowe Center on Forest Street in Hartford, visitors can literally walk into Harriet's life. Built in 1871, the cottage is where Harriet lived during her last two decades and wrote her final works. She died in her upstairs bedroom with several of her children, her sister Isabella Beecher Hooker and other family members by her side. Her husband, Calvin, a retired biblical scholar, had died there ten years earlier.

Many say it's her ghost that causes the house's hardwood floors to creak, window shades in the parlor to open and a gray image to sometimes appear at night in the Visitor Center. But even when paranormal experts from the SyFy television network's Ghost Hunters show spent an evening investigating there, Stowe Center executive director Katherine Kane was more focused on Harriet's life than afterlife.

"Our propensity as people is to look to the future rather than to the past. But looking at the past can help understand where we are and what we might do to make things better," said Kane. "Harriet was a woman who spoke out for what she believed in and provoked people to think, because her writing was simple, straightforward and heartfelt. A lot of writing of the day—especially by abolitionists—was formulaic and preachy. But Harriet wrote in a way that touched people and, maybe most importantly, was able to present issues like slavery in a way that showed they weren't just race issues, they were human issues."

The daughter of Roxanna Foote Beecher and the Reverend Lyman Beecher, Harriet Elisabeth Beecher was born on June 14, 1811, in Litchfield, Connecticut, the sixth of eleven children. Her mother died when Harriet was just five, at which point her eldest sister, Catharine, became a second mother. Fairly quickly, however, Lyman married a widow, Harriet Porter, whose three children, Isabella, Thomas and James, became part of the Beecher brood.

Guided by Lyman, the children were expected to find a purpose, and young Harriet believed hers was to write. First recognition of her potential to succeed at the craft came in the form of a school essay writing prize when she was just seven. Roughly a year before her death, said her obituary in the *New York Times*, Harriet told a reporter that a poem written when she was eight, after her kitten died, was her first real creative work:

Here lies poor Kit,
Who had a fit
And acted queer,
Killed with a gun,
Her race is run,
And she lies here.

The ability to express ideas of all kinds was nurtured—expected even—in the Beecher house. Harriet's father, a religion teacher at Sarah Pierce's Female Academy in Litchfield, Connecticut, expected his children at both school and at home to be lively and effective debaters. He helped ensure Harriet developed this skill by enrolling her at the Sarah Pierce academy, where rather than just learn traditional "ornamental arts" like needlepoint and manners, girls were taught languages, math and history. Writing lessons forced her to analyze and to express herself critically rather than just expressively. It was excellent training ground for an emerging author. Stowe then became a student at the Hartford Female Seminary founded by her sister Catharine. There, she was able to grow and hone her writing abilities and soon began to write for pay, crafting articles, essays and short stories for area newspapers, journals and magazines.

At age twenty-one, she moved to Cincinnati to be with her father, who had been named president of the socially progressive Lane Theological Seminary, which trained Presbyterian ministers. There, she and her sisters attended many of their father's fiery sermons and speeches about the abomination of slavery and the need for social activism. Harriet also joined the Semi-Colon Club, a literary salon and social club that introduced Harriet to widower Calvin Stowe, a professor at the seminary and, like her father, an ardent abolitionist.

Harriet's *New York Times* obituary describes the time like this:

> [It] *was the turning point of her career. Nowhere were the "underground railway" and pathetic incidents under the fugitive slave law more familiar than on the border of Ohio. Nowhere was there a stronger anti-slavery agitation or more flourishing hotbed of abolition than at Lane Seminary...In anticipation of violence, the Stowe residence was armed and equipped with a large bell to summon help. In her husband's house many a fugitive was sheltered and many a thrilling tale rehearsed. Thus, in a sense, "Uncle Tom's Cabin" was not a freak of fancy. Its inspiration and its incidents came from actual life.*

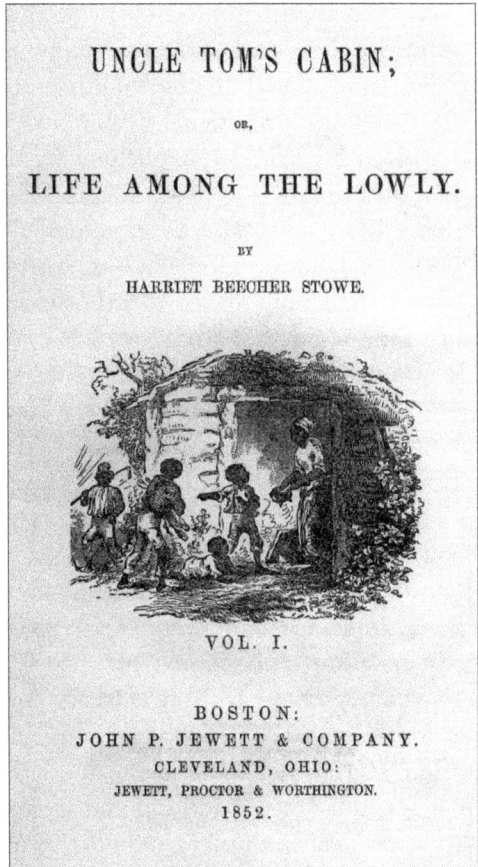

UNCLE TOM'S CABIN;

OR,

LIFE AMONG THE LOWLY.

BY

HARRIET BEECHER STOWE.

VOL. I.

BOSTON:
JOHN P. JEWETT & COMPANY.
CLEVELAND, OHIO:
JEWETT, PROCTOR & WORTHINGTON.
1852.

Title page of the first edition of *Uncle Tom's Cabin*, 1852. *Harriet Beecher Stowe Center, Hartford, Connecticut.*

As the *New York Times* goes on to explain, Harriet and Calvin were active members of the Underground Railroad, hiding and helping coordinate safe passage for slaves escaping from Southern plantations. They also were active in growing their family and, during their time in Cincinnati, had seven children, including twin daughters. But in 1849, sorrow came for thirty-year-old Harriet when her eighteen-month-old son, Samuel, died of cholera.

Today, this intestinal infection primarily affects those living in developing countries, where poor sanitation allows the potentially deadly *Vibrio cholerae* bacterium to spread. In nineteenth-century America, however, it was a too-common illness, causing many parents to feel the devastating anguish that, later in her life, Harriet said helped her understand what slaves experienced when their children were sold: "The bitterest tears shed over graves are for words left unsaid and deeds left undone."

When Calvin was offered a teaching position at his alma mater, Bowdoin College, the family moved to Brunswick, Maine. There, in a rented house at 63 Federal Street, Harriet in 1852 wrote the novel that would change her life and the way people around the world viewed slavery, *Uncle Tom's Cabin*. In 1962, the house was designated a National Historic Landmark. Known as the Harriet Beecher Stowe House, it's owned by Bowdoin College but, unlike her house in Hartford, is not open to the public.

The assignment to write *Uncle Tom's Cabin* came from the publisher of the abolitionist newspaper the *National Era*, who asked Stowe to write a piece that would "paint a word picture of slavery" and run in several installments. Harriet imagined she would write a piece consisting of three or four parts, but it ended up being more than forty.

The story opens with an African American mother named Eliza and her four-year-old son, Harry, running away from a Kentucky plantation to prevent Harry from being sold to another slave owner. For many readers, the image of this mother and son and their desperate plight was their first up-close view of the injustices and horrors of slavery. Other characters Harriet brings to life are the book's namesake, Tom, a religious man who plantation owners sell to help pay their debts; Topsy, a young black slave who uses mischief to hide her pain; Eva, the young daughter of a white slave owner who makes friends with Tom; and, perhaps most memorable, the cruel and violent Simon Legree, who orders that Tom be whipped to death for refusing to deny his faith in God or betray the hiding place of two female runaways.

To write the story, Harriet reached out to friends and family, asking them to send stories they'd heard or read about slaves' flights to freedom. She also read the handful of narratives that had been written by slaves who'd successfully escaped to Canada. But most importantly, she was also able to fall back on her own experiences. Her grandmother had African American servants, several of whom the family suspected were former slaves, and Harriet grew up spending time with all of them. In Cincinnati, her and Calvin's participation in the Underground Railroad also gave her the opportunity to get to know many African Americans on the run from

Harriet in an 1866 edition of *Our Young Folks* illustrated magazine. *Harriet Beecher Stowe Center, Hartford, Connecticut.*

the slave hunters hired by their Southern owners to bring them back dead or alive.

It's also possible that, despite the differences in their looks and lives, Harriet felt a real kinship with the slaves she met. In many respects, 1800s women had much in common with African Americans, and it was common for female abolitionists to be both passionate abolitionists and suffragists. Like women, even free blacks in the North were not allowed to own property or vote. Women were also not allowed to own their own property or keep the income they earned. Married women were considered their husbands' property and unmarried women their fathers'. Although Harriet and Calvin had a more equal marriage and relationship than most couples of the time, many female abolitionists saw their work for civil rights intrinsically linked to women's rights, and undoubtedly Harriet was one of them.

One runaway slave might have even lived in her home for a while. Letters suggest that when she and Calvin discovered that an African American servant working for them might actually be a runaway in danger of being captured, they helped arrange for him to escape to Canada, where he could live in freedom.

Harriet also had strong opinions about Congress' Compromise of 1850, legislation designed to end slave trade but not slavery and created a new and stricter Fugitive Slave Law.

Throughout the United States, helping escaped slaves had been illegal since 1793. But the 1850 law required that everyone, including public citizens, help catch runaways. Those who refused could be fined up to $1,000 and jailed for six months. The law also eliminated what little legal protection runaways once had. Its wording, in fact, made it possible for any African American to be taken from the street, accused of being a fugitive slave and then brought to a federally appointed commissioner who received five dollars for every fugitive wrongly captured and released and ten dollars for every one sent South.

Free African Americans and abolitionists like Harriet were furious about the law, arguing that the system was unjust and immoral, making it profitable for any black person to be captured and forcing those who didn't believe in slavery to support it. Her protest involved not just writing letters to the editor and speaking out to whoever would listen but also hiding runaways in Brunswick. Said Harriet simply, "No one can have the system of slavery brought before him without an irrepressible desire to do something."

Harriet's signature. *Harriet Beecher Stowe Center, Hartford, Connecticut.*

The first installment of *Uncle Tom's Cabin* appeared in the *National Era* on June 5, 1851. The following year, the collected installments were published as a two-volume book, becoming an unprecedented bestseller. In the United States, it sold 10,000 copies in its first week and 300,000 copies in its first year. In England, it sold 1.5 million copies in the first year. Resonating with international audiences, it was also a bestseller in Europe and Asia, for many months being listed in the No. 2 slot. The Bible was No. 1. Over the years, it's been published in more than sixty languages.

A New Home in Hartford

The success of *Uncle Tom's Cabin* brought the Stowes financial security and allowed Harriet to focus on writing full time. Among the first pieces she wrote in that first year following were *Key to Uncle Tom's Cabin*, which reported on the case histories she had used to write the novel, and another antislavery novel called *Dred: A Tale from the Swamp*. These and *Uncle Tom's Cabin* are among the books Harriet is most known for, but it wasn't just civil rights and justice that caused her to take to the page.

The ability to independently and publicly express her beliefs at a time when women were considered their husbands' or fathers' property was something Harriet did not take lightly. Women in the mid-1800s had few rights, so Harriet couldn't vote or hold office. But she could speak her mind, and she said, "The truth is the kindest thing we can give folks in the end."

Among the works she published are children's texts, homemaking and parenting advice books, biographies, analyses that tackle religious reform and gender roles and additional novels. In all, her fifty-one-year writing career led to thirty published books as well as countless short stories, poems, articles and hymns. Almost all her works were popular and sold well, even her more scholarly ones. People, it seems, were drawn to her informal, conversational writing style.

The last several of those works were written in Hartford, where Harriet and Calvin retired after spending eleven years in Andover, Massachusetts. They moved there after Bowdoin, which allowed Calvin to accept a professorship at Andover Theological Seminary. Then, they lived in two homes in Hartford. The first was a Gothic villa that Harriet designed herself and had built in Nook Farm, an exclusive, park-like neighborhood in the west end known for the scholars and artists who lived there. Her neighbors included

An older Harriet. *Library of Congress.*

Civil War general, governor and senator Joseph Hawley and actor William Gillette, who later built Gillette Castle in East Haddam. Industrialization and high costs to maintain the mansion caused her to move in 1873 to the brick cottage on Forest Street, where she lived the last twenty-three years of her life, the final ten without Calvin, who died in 1886.

The Katharine Day House at the Harriet Beecher Stowe Center on Forest Street in Hartford.

Life, however, was far from quiet there. Mark Twain was her neighbor and, in addition to the steady stream of visitors who went between his house and hers, Harriet embarked on two lengthy speaking tours, one that brought her down the East Coast and another that took her to the West. A champion of progressive ideas, she helped reinvigorate interest in the art at the Wadsworth Atheneum, as well as establish the Hartford Art School that is now part of the University of Hartford. Among the books she wrote there were the popular *The American Woman's Home*, *Lady Byron Vindicated* and *Pogunuc People*.

The house was—and still is—full of paintings, portraits, souvenirs and knickknacks, many of which were gifts sent from fans around the world. Paintings created by Harriet herself hang on several walls. There's also a written description of how Harriet saw herself at the time she wrote *Uncle Tom's Cabin*, which was published in an 1896 edition of the *New York Times*: "A little bit of a woman, rather more than forty, as withered and dry as a pinch of snuff, never very well worth looking at in my best days, and now a decidedly used-up article."

Today, her house and the nonprofit Harriet Beecher Stowe Center in Hartford are open to visitors year-round. A stop on the Connecticut Women's

Heritage Trail, the site is open seven days a week, except for major holidays. Several times a year, it also hosts special events. Among them each October is "Spirits at Stowe: An Otherworldly Tour," which allows visitors to explore not only the rooms Harriet lived in but also her interest in the paranormal. Guided tours for schools and groups are also regularly offered, as are lectures and other programs that "provoke people to think, like Harriet did," said the Stowe Center's Katherine Kane.

"Our events follow the topics and issues that were important to Harriet," Kane added. "She started writing as a way to earn money for her family and became a literary rock star who could use her name as leverage to make a difference. She was a woman who was always thinking and wanted to inspire people to work to solve the problems they care about."

Photographs of Harriet are located throughout Hartford's Stowe Center, including those that show her at the end of her life when, said the *New York Times*, "She always had pleasant words for the children of the neighborhood, with whom she talked in her rambles, and seemed to be at her brightest when thinking of and talking with them." In that same feature published the day after her death, the *Times* also said:

> *The death of Harriet Beecher Stowe is more than the ending of a woman's life of whatever degree of fame. It marks the extinction of genius in a family, and is one of the closing leaves in an era of our century. The more famous children of a famous father leave worthy descendants, but none of their own mental gifts or rank. Rarely, indeed, is there so much in a single life so memorable or so interesting as in that of the writer of probably the most widely read work of fiction ever penned.*

Harriet Beecher Stowe: a remarkable woman and role model for yesterday and today.

Chapter 4

ELIZABETH COLT

FIRST LADY OF HARTFORD: 1826–1905

Old newspaper articles praise Elizabeth Colt for having a "gentle character," performing "good works" and being "the friend of all who knew her." She's probably best known for being the wife of Colt firearms inventor and manufacturer Samuel Colt. But Elizabeth was more than the woman who took over and ran Sam's gun empire for thirty-nine years after he suddenly and tragically died. As progressive as the era she lived in, she was first president of the Hartford Soldiers Aid Society, an organizer of Connecticut's first women's suffrage convention, the benefactor and founder of the Church of the Good Shepherd, a patron of countless charities and the donor of a vast wing and art collection at the Wadsworth Atheneum.

Elizabeth's work as a businesswoman, art patron, civic leader and philanthropist earned her the title of "First Lady of Hartford." When she died in August 1905, *Hartford Courant* editors honored her in a way they had never honored any woman before, dedicating an entire front page to her life, death and impact on the community:

> *It would hardly be possible to overestimate the importance of Mrs. Colt's position in the life of this city. The outward signs of it remain in the beautiful home with its spacious grounds, a place beloved by her for its tender associations…The news of [her] death will cause much regret in this city and elsewhere, where she was much esteemed for her fine character, abiding faith and philanthropic deeds…Hartford sustains an irreparable*

Portrait of a young Elizabeth, painted by Richard Morrell Staigg in 1856, the year she married Samuel. A lock of her hair is encased in the frame. *Wadsworth Atheneum Museum of Art/Art Resource, New York.*

loss in her death. Among all classes and conditions of people in the community, her sincere mourners will be found. She has become our most remarkable woman.

A Life of Privilege and Sorrow

The eldest child of the Reverend William and Elizabeth Hart Jarvis, Elizabeth Hart Colt was born on October 5, 1826, in Saybrook, Connecticut. Her father was a well-known Episcopal minister and her mother part of a prominent Rhode Island family that included several English royal governors and military leaders. Business and trade with the West Indies made them extremely wealthy, so money was not what Elizabeth was looking for in a husband.

In 1856, Elizabeth married Sam. The two met five years earlier in Newport, Rhode Island, and by all accounts, it was a true love. They were inseparable soul mates, devoted to creating a partnership. For their honeymoon, they spent a year abroad, traveling throughout Germany, England and Russia, as well as attending the coronation of Russia's Czar Alexander II at the Moscow Kremlin. They came home to Armsmear, a massive pink stone villa with round arches and iron balconies that Sam built for Elizabeth as a wedding present on property overlooking the Colt Armory. The couple planned to spend a lifetime there, but it lasted just five years. At forty-seven, Sam died suddenly in January 1862. The *New York Times* reported that he suffered "an acute attack upon the brain" after being ill for several days.

Elizabeth buried Sam on the grounds of Armsmear, near where she had already created graves for three of their children, two who died in infancy and a seven-month-old who died just ten days after Sam. She watched his casket be buried from her boudoir window, writing, "I see the workmen at the tomb, preparing a last resting place for him. It seems as if the main spring is broken and the works must run down."

Her fifth baby, with whom Elizabeth was newly pregnant when Sam died, was born stillborn the following July. Only her beloved son Caldwell survived, but Elizabeth eventually buried him too. A business investor and yachtsman, he reportedly died of tonsillitis when he was thirty-six.

Sam's death made Elizabeth, only thirty-five, one of the richest women in the United States. Colt's Patent Arms Manufacturing Company was the largest firearms manufacturer in the world, and Sam's will left her (unheard of at the time) controlling interest. Between the business, their home and other assets, she had inherited roughly $200 million by today's rates but also, as her obituary in the *Hartford Courant* read, "heavy responsibility."

The only true way to honor and keep Sam's memory alive was to ensure that Colt Manufacturing survived by meeting massive orders for guns that needed to be filled. The Civil War was underway, and Sam had committed

Elizabeth with her beloved son Caldwell, painted in 1865 by Charles Loring Elliot.
Wadsworth Atheneum Museum of Art/Art Resource, New York.

to producing his precise and sleek revolvers for Northern troops. He cut off all sales to the South once war was officially declared. Under Elizabeth's leadership, every one of those Union orders was met on time. Like Sam, she demanded a high standard of precision manufacturing and, though she

Elizabeth's signature, 1875. *Harriet Beecher Stowe Center, Hartford, Connecticut.*

never served officially as president, guided the business through its greatest period of prosperity from 1870 to 1890.

Even when the Colt Armory burned to the ground in the midst of the Civil War, and Elizabeth watched from her bedroom window as her husband's dreams turned to ruins, she persevered—though not without heartache, as her father recorded: "To think that the magnificent, noble structure is in ruins…it seems so identified with [Sam]. It seems like burying him again…Elizabeth bears it…with calmness…When the beautiful dome fell, she burst into tears."

Rumor was that Confederate sympathizers had torched the building. It was never proven, but Elizabeth had the choice of rebuilding or taking the approximately $17 million in insurance money and moving on. Her choice: rebuild. The decision would ensure the continuation of her husband's legacy, as well as guarantee that the Northern army continued to receive much-needed guns and ammunition supplies.

Carefully designed to look much like the original armory complete with its Russian-influenced, onion-shaped blue dome, the new armory was larger and contained more practical elements. The layout was more streamlined. It included a fourth and extra floor, but maybe most importantly, it was built, at Elizabeth's insistence, to be as fireproof as possible.

Tremendous growth followed, and by the height of the Civil War, the company that Sam started with 50 people had expanded to more than 1,400. With Elizabeth at the helm, accomplishments over the next four decades included the development of several new guns, including a new revolver known as the "Peacemaker" and used widely throughout the West, as well as a gas-operated, air-cooled machine gun that played a major role in the Spanish-American War.

She sold the business in 1901 when she was seventy-five.

Role as "First Lady"

Like many across the United States in the years leading up to the start of the twentieth century, Elizabeth felt a strong sense of urgency to help Hartford recover from the Civil War and the accompanying poverty that had affected so many lives. The Reverend E.P. Parker of Hartford's South Congregational Church wrote about her contributions to the community in one of the tributes the *Courant* published after her death:

> *She was nobody's enemy, she was everybody's friend. With strong convictions and decided opinions, she combined utmost courtesy and kindness. Through long years of residence here, her benignity and beneficence have gone together, hand in hand, in all the public or private ways that connect charity with necessities, or afford the opportunity of the ministrations of loving kindness. Who that has ever seen the light of her countenance will ever forget it?*

Generous, compassionate, forward thinking: Undoubtedly, Elizabeth Colt was and still stands as the greatest philanthropist in Hartford's history. Touching and improving countless lives along the way, she built parks, a church, social service organizations, part of an art museum and a legacy that will last as long as Hartford stands. For this work, she was dubbed the "First Lady of Hartford," and the list of her countless contributions proves why. Included in her most public volunteer efforts are twenty-two years as president of the Union for Home Work, which provided working mothers with daycare, meals, classes and access to a library; serving as first president of the Hartford Soldiers Aid Society, which was responsible for overseeing the efforts and activities of seventy local charities; organizing Connecticut's first women's suffrage convention in 1869; and founding the Church of the Good Shepherd. Her vision was that this magnificent Gothic church would be a place where she, Armsmear neighbors and Colt Armory employees could gather and worship together. The church was consecrated in 1869. When her son Caldwell died, she built a nearby three-story parish house and community center to honor his memory. When she died, her will included a trust to help provide for the church's continuing maintenance and ministry.

With the help of noted nineteenth-century painter and fellow Hartfordite Frederic Church, Elizabeth also created on the second floor of Armsmear the first public art and picture gallery in the nation. Among the works, which can now be viewed at the Wadsworth Atheneum, are several of Church's

The onion-shaped dome at the top of the former Colt Armory building is a Hartford landmark visible from Interstate 91. *Detroit Publishing Company Photograph Collection, Library of Congress.*

pastoral landscapes, a popular style during the Victorian period. In her will, she also bequeathed $50,000 to build a wing to house the more than one thousand items the atheneum received upon her death. These also can be viewed and include jewelry, sculptures, tapestries, furniture, guns from Sam's personal collection, gifts given to the Colts by Czar Alexander II and, perhaps most touching, an elaborate hand-carved wooden cradle that Elizabeth only too briefly used.

Spending time with these items provides an intimate, bittersweet and remarkable window into Elizabeth and Sam Colt's world. "Elizabeth had her hands in almost every progressive movement of her time—the women's movement, a commission working to improve sanitation, supporting the end of slavery," said Wadsworth Atheneum associate curator Alyce Perry Englund. "She had such devastation in her life with the death of her husband and children, yet she refused to succumb to grief and flourished in Sam's shadow. She was a leader in Sam's business, a patron of charities throughout the city and, when you look at how she persevered after the armory fire, she was literally a phoenix who came out of the ashes."

Perhaps the most visible aspects of Elizabeth and Sam's lasting influence and impact in Hartford today is the Coltsville Historic District off Wethersfield Avenue, which in 2008 became a National Historic Landmark District. Within it are the several Colt properties also listed on the National Register of Historic Places, including the Colt Armory; several factory buildings, including the machine shop and warehouse; the cottage-like houses where workers lived; and, of course, Armsmear, which at Elizabeth's request was converted into a home for widows of Episcopal ministers as part of the terms of her will. She gave the grounds surrounding Armsmear to the City of Hartford to create Colt Park. When Elizabeth lived there, included in its 140 acres were exquisitely manicured lawns, extensive gardens, lush greenhouses and a pond. Today, the pond is still there, as well as a tiered fountain. But ball fields, playgrounds and picnic areas have also been added. Standing tall and overlooking it all is a statue of Sam that Elizabeth commissioned with a plaque that reads: "Samuel Colt, 1814–1862. On the grounds on which his taste beautified by the home he loved, this memorial stands to speak of his genius, his enterprise, and of his great and loyal heart."

A Heartfelt Goodbye

Two weeks after leaving Hartford in what the *Courant* said was "especially good health," seventy-nine-year-old Elizabeth Colt died in August 1905 in Newport, Rhode Island, after being "stricken with paralysis" while visiting a niece. The front-page article notes that less than a year before, Elizabeth had traveled to Boston to attend the General Convention of Episcopal Churches, taking an active role in the triennial meeting of the Woman's Auxiliary. Just a month before, she had spent time in New Milford at a Bible and mission study, as well as time on her son Caldwell's yacht, the *Dauntess*, which she "fitted as a house-boat" and docked in nearby Essex.

Her body was brought back to Hartford for funeral services in the Church of the Good Shepherd that she helped found, where longtime Colt employees carried her casket. She was buried at Hartford's Cedar Hill Cemetery, under a soaring Egyptian-style monument of pink Scotch and Westerly granite, topped with the angel Gabriel holding a horn, symbolic of the last triumph. At the time of Caldwell's death, she had Sam and their babies disinterred from their burial place at Armsmear and moved to Cedar Hill, so that when

Elizabeth's obituary took up the entire front page of the August 24, 1905 *Hartford Courant*. It was the first time the *Courant* recognized a woman's death this way. *Hartford Courant.*

The Colt monument sits on a hill at Cedar Hill Cemetery, located off Fairfield Avenue in Hartford.

51

the time came, she could lay between Sam and Caldwell. She also asked that the caskets of three of her infants be placed with her in her grave.

One of the many people who wrote letters to the *Courant* in response to Elizabeth's death was a woman listed as Mrs. F.W. Cheney, who said:

> *There are but few men or women whose departure from earth leaves in the community they have lived in a sense of emptiness, an aching void which no other presence can fill. Mrs. Colt was one of those few. Hartford has been her larger home, a community thoroughly conscious of her influence, and where her presence has been like that of a wise mother in her household, uniting, shaping, controlling the social springs of life, quieting discord, evoking harmony out of contrary elements, bestowing a hallowed sympathy on aching hearts, dispensing a noble and gracious hospitality. Her womanhood has been a wonderful blend of dignity and gentle simplicity. It has never been necessary for her to feign a kindness she did not feel, since it was as natural to her to be kind as to breathe. Nor did this mean a weak or undiscriminating judgment. Her standards were high and were applied as directly to others as to herself...It is worthwhile for all of us who have loved her and who mourn for her to reflect a little upon the breadth and depth of the influence which emanated from one who so little sought it.*

In the months following Elizabeth's death, many who paid tribute to this courageous, giving and remarkable woman commented on how everyone in Hartford knew and would always remember her. The same should be true today.

Chapter 5

VIRGINIA THRALL SMITH

PIONEERING CHILDREN'S RIGHTS ACTIVIST:
1836–1903

The first few paragraphs of a November 5, 1995 *Hartford Courant* op-ed piece about nineteenth-century children's advocate Virginia Thrall Smith is worth reading word by word:

> *"If we merely tell them coldly and reprovingly to go to work, we give them a stone; but if we give them human sympathy and help them into a place where their work will feed them, we give them bread."*
>
> *These words, spoken by city missionary Virginia Thrall Smith on a Sunday evening in 1883 to an annual public gathering of the City Missionary Society of Hartford, were delivered in an effort to raise money for the poor who, many believed, should have been forced to help themselves.*
>
> *Welfare reform was a heated topic in this country during the last quarter of the 19th century, and the discourse does not appear to have been radically different from our own today.*
>
> *More than 100 years ago, the debate raged about what to do with the increasing numbers of abused, neglected and orphaned children suffering from the ravaging effects of drug and alcohol addiction by their parents. At that time, crime, joblessness, poverty, addictions and teen pregnancy were linked, as today, with the inevitable consequence of child abuse.*
>
> *In Hartford, welfare reform focused on Smith and the social programs she generated from her position with the Hartford City Missionary Society, a charitable organization supported by the Congregational churches of the city. Smith and her contemporaries saw depression and disease fester in*

Perhaps the most well-known photograph of Virginia, taken at mid-life. *Butterworth family.*

tenements, while crimes and poverty escalated in the new urban environments. They observed a cycle of poverty emerging and warned of the detrimental effects to future generations if action was not taken.

The piece was written by West Hartford resident and social worker Linda Smith Cohen, who, despite the shared name, is not related to Virginia. And as Cohen notes in her commentary, if Virginia Thrall Smith were alive today, she'd sadly and perhaps even bewilderingly see that even though it's now the twenty-first century, little has changed since she gave that speech on that 1880s Sunday night. The handful of differences between then and now include the fact that the Hartford City Missionary Society no longer exists—though the brick building Virginia oversaw the organization move in to, most recognizable by its pyramid-shaped tower, still stands at 234 Pearl Street. Also, at least in the United States, the term "orphan" has for the most part gone out of style, and tenements are now more commonly referred to as housing complexes. But crime, joblessness, poverty, addiction and "the inevitable consequence of child abuse" are still among the most pressing—and poisonous—problems society faces today. Yet this reality should not in any way suggest that Virginia and her dedicated corps of volunteers did not make a difference in the lives of countless children and families throughout Hartford and beyond.

The founder of the first free kindergarten program in Connecticut in 1881 at the Hartford City Missionary Society, Virginia worked tirelessly for children, not just advocating for the educational and social services she believed children and their families deserved, but envisioning what those services should be.

"Today we have laws that protect children. But when Virginia Thrall Smith was alive, none of those laws existed," said Galo Rodriguez, president and CEO of Hartford's Village for Children and Families.

Indeed, at the time of Virginia's first kindergarten, school for children of any age was considered more of a nicety than a necessity. Attending school was optional until 1899, the year Connecticut enacted the law that made it mandatory for all children between seven and sixteen years old. Virginia, however, saw the need for early childhood education more than a decade before, particularly for children living in unstable or unhealthy home environments.

"Her vision and leadership provided the first semblance of a system designed to help children in crisis and, more importantly," Galo continued, "to prevent those crises from occurring in the first place."

Mother, Missionary, Champion

The daughter of Hiram and Melissa Crawford Thrall, Virginia was born in 1836 in Bloomfield, Connecticut, and went to school at the Suffield Institute, as well as attended the Hartford Female Seminary founded and run by Harriet Beecher Stowe's eldest sister, Catharine. She then attended Mount Holyoke Female Seminary in Massachusetts, now Mount Holyoke College, and on New Year's Eve 1857, she married tailor and clothes dealer William Smith. She was twenty-one.

Virginia earned a diploma from the Hartford Female Seminary, a progressive school that, in addition to academics, offered girls twelve and up "radical" programs like physical education. *Wikimedia Commons, public domain.*

The two moved to Hartford and had six children. Three of them— Lucy, Edward and Kate—died from diphtheria in infancy. Perhaps it was the result of these personal tragedies that led Smith to become such a passionate champion for the health, well being and happiness of all children, rich and poor.

With the backing and urging of the Reverend Dr. Nathaniel Burton, pastor of Hartford's Park Congregational Church, Virginia in December 1876 became administrator of the Hartford City Mission, an organization that worked to provide poor families with "comfort, guidance and resources." According to Virginia's obituary in the January 5, 1903 *Hartford Courant*, Reverend Burton had "long known of her private charities and labors in the interests of the poor." Headquarters for the mission was in an "inadequate," unused storefront, but Virginia took on her new responsibilities with "energy and a true sense of duty," the *Courant* continued, writing, "She at once put into practice the theory that the best way to help the poor was to teach them to help themselves and, in this spirit, she instituted a loan system, whereby self-respecting persons might obtain small sums to meet their most pressing wants."

Her work focused on empowering the poor with skills they could both earn money from and take pride in and led to her opening a school that

Virginia's home at the corner of Farmington Avenue and Imlay Street in Hartford. *Butterworth family.*

taught women how to do laundry and cook, as well as establishing programs like the Women's Sewing Class and Reading Society, Singing School for Girls and a Boys Club Flower Mission.

The results of these programs and others exceeded Hartford leaders' expectations. Perhaps one of her most significant accomplishment, however, was the creation of Connecticut's first free kindergarten at the mission, followed by the founding of the Free Kindergarten Association. Its thirty-three volunteer members were responsible for overseeing this new schooling option. They and Virginia also lobbied the Connecticut General Assembly to craft the legislation needed to establish kindergartens in Connecticut public schools. The bill passed unanimously.

The accomplishment, coupled with continued efforts to improve young children's access to much-needed education and healthcare, led to Virginia being invited to speak at the weeklong 1893 World's Congress of Representative Women at the Chicago World's Fair. It was an event designed to bring together "some of the most important assemblages of women the world" working to make "a greater future for the human race." Attended by more than 150,000 people, it featured speeches by almost 500 women, including "The Kindergarten: Fresh Air Work and Family Homes for Children" given by Virginia.

An excerpt from Virginia's address was included in a special World's Fair book published by the Congress of Women. For people today who've never thought to imagine a time when there were no kindergartens or preschools, the ideas she presented for an organized educational program for children as young as two and a half seem just what they are: outdated. But seven years before the start of the twentieth century, they were truly visionary.

> *Every community stands under a moral obligation to give to every helpless child born within its borders the best possible chance to grow into honesty and virtue...*[Kindergarten provides] *happy entertainment, wise development and instruction for little heads, hands and hearts, and with many a motherly lesson in cleanliness...*
>
> *...We must begin in the right way to educate the children of the very poor. We must pick up out of the swearing alleys and gutters of depraved neighborhoods the neglected, harshly treated, half-fed and half-clothed, unwashed and uncombed prattling child, whose greatest knowledge of language is of slang and profanity, cleanse it and cover it with wholesome garments; teach it how to play and how to talk and what truth is, and so, lovingly and carefully, plant the germ of good in its receptive mind, and fill its hopeful heart with happy dreams of doing something noble in the future that the results must be beneficial to a great degree to the race we are trying to save.*
>
> *It is a higher duty of society to prevent crime than to punish it. The one is ennobling and pleasant and the other harsh and deterrent.*

A Statewide Role

Virginia's ever-growing focus on the poor led to her being appointed a member of the Connecticut State Board of Charities. As such, she visited the state poorhouses and poor farms, where homeless adults and children lived and worked in cramped and too often unclean, unhealthy and what Virginia saw as deplorable conditions.

Enraged, Virginia petitioned the legislature to abolish the practice of sending abandoned, neglected or parentless children to these facilities. Similar to today's foster care system, the resulting law that passed provided the establishment of clean and safe temporary homes but only for needy children without physical or emotional disabilities. For "the incurables"—children whose physical, emotional or behavioral health seemed less than ideal—the poorhouse was still their only option.

Virginia's signature, 1875. *Harriet Beecher Stowe Center, Hartford, Connecticut.*

Virginia was disappointed with this half victory, and shortly after, disaster struck. Her work helping unwed mothers find homes and medical care during their pregnancies led to loud claims by conservatives that Virginia was encouraging immoral behavior. Louder and even more damaging were accusations that instead of helping these mothers find foster and adoptive care for their newborns, Virginia was actually involved in baby farming, taking payments for the babies' care and sale. A horrified Virginia insisted on her innocence, and no claims were ever proven. But the doubt and dark mark they caused forced Virginia to resign from the Hartford City Mission.

Determined to continue her work, she and her followers formed the Connecticut Children's Aid Society and purchased a house in Wethersfield to care for sick and abandoned children. Neighbors protested the facility, but Virginia persevered and, a year later, in 1896, attempted to found a second, similar home in Plainville. Plainville officials blocked her plans, as did those in Hartford, who said the house she wanted was too close to the trolley line and that trolley riders would find seeing the children too distressing.

In 1898, however, Virginia found success and land in Newington on a fifty-six-acre working farm. Children would live in the farmhouse, and children and staff would work together to raise chickens, cows and other animals for milk, meat and eggs, as well as grow their own vegetables. By 1901, a second building was needed to comfortably house the forty-one children living there. Today, that facility is the 187-bed, nonprofit Connecticut Children's Medical Center, which, in addition to caring for some of the sickest children in New England, is the primary teaching hospital for pediatricians training at the University of Connecticut School of Medicine.

Virginia's Connecticut Children's Aid Society has evolved into Rodriguez's Village for Families and Children, which provides foster care, accredited

MRS. VIRGINIA T. SMITH.

DEATH OF A FORMER CITY MISSIONARY AND ALMONER.

Prominently Identified with Children's Aid Society—Mother of Dr. O. C. Smith and W. B. Smith, the Actor.

Mrs. Virginia T. Smith, for many years missionary of the City Missionary Society, and during her active life identified with charitable organizations in the city and the state, died at her home, No. 621 Farmington avenue, at 3:45 o'clock Saturday morning. Mrs. Smith's death had been expected for the past few weeks, as she had been in failing health for several months. About a

Virginia's obituary in the *Hartford Courant*, January 5, 1903. *Hartford Courant.*

behavioral health and social services and other programs to as many as 8,200 children a year.

"Virginia gave a voice to those who weren't being heard and believed that with the proper opportunities, education and nurturing, anyone can make it. She believed in people's desire to succeed," Galo Rodriguez continued, "and that every person has within them the capacity to succeed if given the needed tools. It's work we strive to continue by providing integrated services and, like Virginia, doing as much as we can with what we have."

Envisioning the Future

Those today who know of Virginia mostly associate her with the establishment of early education and child welfare services. But as Linda Smith Cohen wrote in her op-ed piece, Virginia's recognition of the multigenerational damage caused by drug and alcohol addiction was also ahead of its time. It led to her establishing both youth substance abuse and prevention programs. To quote Linda, who researched Virginia for her master's thesis in American Studies at Trinity College, "She believed the future depended on it."

At a time when races and classes were clearly divided, Virginia was also willing to use her voice to remind others that difference should be a reason for celebration rather than discrimination. She also believed people should make a conscious effort to allow themselves to "be filled with a sense of our common humanity," said ninety-five-year-old Miriam "Mims"

Painting by C.R. Loomis of an older Virginia that hangs in the administrative offices of the Village for Families and Children in Hartford.

Butterworth of Bloomfield, Connecticut, whose late husband, Oliver Butterworth, was Virginia's great-grandson.

"One of the many extraordinary things Virginia did was show women that they could work outside of the home, and that they could do it because they wanted to, rather than because they had to," said Mims, adding that her father-in-law, Paul Butterworth, often talked about his grandmother. "She also was a woman who carried on, no matter what. The accusations of baby farming destroyed her reputation enough that she had to leave the

City Mission, but she didn't let them stop her work. Instead of going home, closing the doors and dying in shame, she organized. She moved forward."

Virginia died in her home on Farmington Avenue in January 1903 after a long illness. "She suffered greatly during her illness, but bore up with fortitude and patience," said her obituary, which shared that she "possessed a natural gift for writing and often contributed stories and short sketches to the daily papers." Even in the last weeks of her life, she worked from home, "keeping up her interest in every detail, arranging and planning for the development of the various branches of philanthropic work," the article reported.

"She was an organizer and had the ability to inspire people into action," added Mims. "I wish I had the chance to know her." No doubt many others today feel the same way, too.

Chapter 6

DOTHA BUSHNELL HILLYER

FORWARD-THINKING FOUNDER OF THE BUSHNELL: 1843–1932

L oving daughter Dotha Bushnell Hillyer envisioned Hartford's Horace Bushnell Memorial Hall, now best known as simply The Bushnell, to be a loving, "living" tribute to the father she idolized, the Reverend Horace Bushnell. Since its opening in January 1930, more than 25 million people have walked through its doors. Yet few know more about the progressive, passionate, turn-of-the-century philanthropist responsible for its construction than her recognizable last name. Fewer still know how this compassionate public servant also led efforts to establish free public high schools in Hartford, as well as was a vocal advocate for improving the despicable conditions of tenement apartments crammed with immigrants and local poor.

Named after her paternal grandmother, Dotha grew up at time when wealth and social class very much determined how a young woman spent her days and what she might achieve. Higher education for women had become more acceptable and, in families like Dotha's, greatly encouraged. By 1880, as many as one-third of American college students were women, but only those who didn't get married were expected to put their educations to use outside the home. Married women were expected to take care of their homes, husbands and children, though gradually it was becoming more acceptable for women—especially those who trained to become teachers or nurses—to work out in the community.

Dotha's marriage at thirty-six to wealthy banker Appleton Hillyer gave her the ability to travel and spend most days as she pleased. With family and friends, she spent carefree summers in Maine and extensively traveled abroad. But

Young Dotha with one of her daughters. *Virginia Hilyard.*

nowhere, it seems, was she more comfortable than home in Hartford, where memories of her father were most strong. Guided by her father, she had also already become an active public servant, giving her time, energy and what would later be discovered as a hidden business expertise to the community.

"To understand Dotha, you first have to understand Horace, because his influence on her was so great," said The Bushnell executive vice-president Ronna Reynolds. "Horace Bushnell was one of the great theologians of the nineteenth century and, really, one of the founders of modern Protestantism. He was also a tremendous Renaissance man. He went to Yale, was highly educated in all areas, was an inventor responsible for the first public water system in Hartford, a consultant on the Transcontinental Railroad, wrote books and articles, was friends with some of the greatest minds of the time, and conceived the idea for what would become the first, large, central public park in the U.S.—Hartford's Bushnell Park."

"While he was doing all these things," Ronna continued, "he was also a crusader for children's rights, African American rights and free high school–level public education, and Dotha lived with him until she was thirty-three and he died. The two of them were inseparable, which means he had just as giant an influence on Dotha as he did on Hartford."

Dotha's father, the Reverend Dr. Horace Bushnell, was clearly the most influential person in her life. She created the Bushnell Center for the Performing Arts in Hartford as a "living memorial" to him. *Virginia Hilyard.*

Her Father's Daughter

The youngest daughter of the Reverend Bushnell and his wife, Mary Apthorpe, Dotha—or Dottie, as her father called her—was born in Hartford in 1843. Little is known about her younger life, though shortly after her father's death in 1876, she decided to "permit myself the egotism" to write down memories of times the two shared. It's a short composition written in tight, slanted script on folded, lined paper that tells about their "peculiarly blessed companionship" during trips to Lake George, Virginia and other locations, which made up "among the dearest recollections of my life" with her father. She also lists several of the small, bittersweet moments they shared during the last year of his life:

> *How often I heard him in his study, earnestly praying that he might be permitted to live to finish his book. In the Spring of 1875, he had the terrible illness which was really a part of this last one that has taken*

him from us…and said farewells to each of us, thinking for two or three days that he was dying. He said to me, "Dottie, I shall never forget you. I love you very much." Early in that sickness, we tried to persuade him to take at least his breakfast in bed, but he said, "No. I want to eat my breakfast with my boots on," and afterwards he insisted upon having thick leather shoes instead of slippers, saying that it made him feel more like a man.

I remember two delightful walks with him in his beloved park, but then… he began visibly to lose ground. On the 28ᵗʰ of January toward twilight, I played with him his last game of backgammon. He proposed it himself, but was too feeble for more than one game. I gratified him by sewing a new black ribbon bow onto his fur cap…but he never went out after that day…I sat by his bed and stroked his hair and…[remembered when] he had taken my face in his hands and playfully shaken it back and forth…The moment he died, I never felt more strongly what a revealer of character the face is. For then, after the spirit had been an hour flown, all the dignity, strength and belovedness of his nature were stamped upon his look in a wonderful and inspiring expression.

Three years later, Dotha married Appleton Robbins Hillyer, one of the founders of Hartford's Aetna National Bank and who had made considerable profits buying, and then later selling, land in the West after the Civil and Mexican-American Wars. During their marriage, Dotha and Appleton established the philanthropic Hillyer Foundation, and the couple became well-known patrons of dozens of local charities, including giving $50,000 to found a night school that eventually evolved into Hillyer College and, in the 1950s, became part of the University of Hartford.

Educational and religious organizations received much of the Hillyers' attention. They gave generous donations to several African American colleges and were principle benefactors of the Science Museum for Children in West Hartford. Now known as the Children's Museum, it's the fifth-oldest children's museum in the nation. The two also gifted more than $50,000 to help build and then support the Hartford YMCA, and they were regular and major contributors to the Windsor Congregational Church, which, when it merged with the Fourth Congregational Church, renamed itself the Horace Bushnell Congregational Church in thanks for Dotha and Appleton's patronage. The church is now the Liberty Christian Center.

Living downtown near Bushnell Park, the couple had three daughters: Catherine, Lucy and Mary. Catherine died in infancy, and Dotha seems to have spent most of Mary and Lucy's young years at home with them. As they got older, however, Dotha began to follow the same path of community service as her father.

"I really believe that like Horace, Dotha was a visionary," said Dotha's great-granddaughter Virginia Hilyard, a Connecticut resident and teacher who feels passionately about keeping Dotha's memory alive. "She questioned, she explored and she believed in giving to her very core. She had deep spiritual beliefs and really was an astute business woman."

She also was a woman who knew what she wanted. *Four Vintage Decades* by Albert W. Coote, a book about The Bushnell's first forty years, includes a description

Dotha was a huge proponent of reading and education, advocating for the establishment of free public high schools. *Bushnell Center for the Performing Arts, Hartford, Connecticut.*

by Dotha's daughter Mary about how Dotha contacted Corbett, Harrison & MacMurray, the architectural firm that had designed New York City's Radio City Music Hall and that she wanted to design The Bushnell too:

> *Being simple and straightforward in her ways, she wrote direct for an appointment with Harvey Wiley Corbett. Mr. Corbett, accustomed to dealing with committees and to drawing plans in competition with other architects, went home that evening to tell his wife that he had had a strange experience. He said that a little old lady had called on him, asked him to build a "large" auditorium in Hartford, and seemed really to mean it.*

Dotha—that "little old lady"—absolutely did. After years of consideration and what turned out to be an inspirational visit to see the Philadelphia

Dotha's signature. *Bushnell Center for the Performing Arts, Hartford, Connecticut.*

Orchestra perform at the Municipal Auditorium in Springfield, Massachusetts, Dotha decided in 1919 to invest $800,000 into the creation of what Coote described as "a gracious architectural memorial to her father." Called the Horace Bushnell Memorial Hall, the building would be located near Dotha's house and across from Bushnell Park and be designed to best express the educational, cultural and civic ideas her father loved. The exact wording in Dotha's will was that it be "suitable for concerts and other musical entertainments, large and small; lectures; civic, political or religious meetings; and other similar activities, including industrial and school exhibitions, fairs and receptions."

Funds for the hall were placed in an investment account as planning got underway, but Dotha, now in her seventies, became seriously ill. That and other commitments led to the project sitting on hold for a decade, but the delay turned out to be fortuitous. Interest and the economic boom of the 1920s caused Dotha's investment to triple, increasing her initial $800,000 investment to $2.5 million. The account was liquidated in 1928 to pay for construction that had just begun and, again, the timing couldn't have been more right. Had the project stayed on hold for just one more year, every cent would have been lost in the Stock Market Crash of 1929.

"The extra funds allowed The Bushnell to be designed with every innovation, including raised floors for the audience, which were brand new at the time. The acoustics are also so ideal that when the auditorium opened, conductors called it the greatest hall in the world," Ronna Reynolds said.

Commitment to a Greater Good

But as a public servant, Dotha wasn't just concerned with how people would experience Bushnell Hall. She was also concerned with what they would experience there. As a devout Christian and minister's daughter, teetering morals were something Dotha was raised to watch out for and not allow in herself or others. This meant that when she noticed that the number of burlesque halls in Hartford was growing, she did not approve. As Ronna explains, what Dotha wanted at The Bushnell was what she had long wanted residents of Hartford to limit themselves to: "wholesome entertainment." For years, in fact, she used her energy to involve herself in the "activities of a Christian woman," said the January 1933 issue of *The Bushnell Prompter*

playbill, which included her fighting to prohibit any more burlesque halls from opening in Hartford and to make prostitution illegal.

A member of the Hartford Parks Board, she was also active in the Civic Club, Saturday Morning Club and founding vice-president of the Municipal Aid Society. Through the Civic Club, she was a driving force in the founding and running of the Hartford School of Housekeeping, which was meant to "improve conditions of domestic service in Hartford" by teaching women how to "properly" cook, waitress, do laundry, market and sew.

She also helped established a night high school for fourteen- to sixteen-year-olds who worked full time to help support their families and couldn't go to school during the day. Against the norm

Dotha and her husband, Appleton, in Maine. *Virginia Hilyard.*

of the day, she also encouraged young women, as well as men, to attend. As more immigrants from Ireland, Italy and other European countries arrived in Hartford, she was part of the committee that ensured that the school added English classes, as well as that students were taught the proper way to write business and social letters. In 1906, Dotha presented the graduation address.

A member of Hartford's Tenement House Committee, Dotha also fought long and sometimes bitter fights to improve sanitation in the city's low-rent apartment buildings, where she found "the evils of congested tenement regions demoralizing to both body and soul."

Dotha was also responsible for the creation of Hartford's Recreation and Public Parks departments, as well as was founding vice-president of the Municipal Art Society formed to "conserve and enhance in every practical way the beauty of the streets, buildings and public places of Hartford." Said an article in *The Bushnell Prompter* playbill shortly after Dotha's death, "All thoughtful people give praise to Him, who directs all lives, for the gift of the personality of Mrs. Hillyer to this city, and for the many gifts which have through her been lavished upon a glad and grateful community."

A Permanent Place in the Community

With her house catty-corner from where The Bushnell was being built, Dotha was able to watch what would become her most well-known and heartfelt public work take shape and, two years later, become fully formed. Sadly, when The Bushnell opened in 1930, she was too ill to attend any of the dedication performances. Among them was a concert by the Philadelphia Orchestra, whose performance more than a decade earlier had convinced her that an auditorium was the tribute she wanted for her father.

Dotha attended just one performance at The Bushnell. During others, she'd watch from her windows, anxious to see the crowds arrive and leave. What she couldn't see, however, was that this grand and much-used building would do more than preserve her father's legacy. It would preserve hers as well.

"I see Dotha's legacy as a continuation of her father's, which includes a reminder to always have your eyes turned to the world, so you don't miss any ideas or innovations that you might bring home to make your community a better place," said Ronna, adding that after Dotha died at eighty-nine in

An older Dotha. *Bushnell Center for the Performing Arts, Hartford, Connecticut.*

December 1932, The Bushnell hosted a memorial service. Every seat in the 2,800-seat auditorium was filled.

"Horace taught Dotha to give your heart to your city, and that's what she did," Ronna continued. "The result was a city that loved her. Her service, compassion and willingness to work to make a difference made her a role model for all women to follow." They also make her a remarkable role model for women today.

Chapter 7

MARY TOWNSEND SEYMOUR

CIVIL RIGHTS CHAMPION: 1873–1957

S he was said to possess a "majesty" when she entered a room and, in 1920, was the first African American woman in the United States to run for a state office. Her grave at Hartford's Old North Cemetery is a stop on the Connecticut Freedom Trail, yet it's generally unkempt—overgrown with poison ivy most of the summer and fall—and on the headstone, no death date has been engraved. She stood up for unfairly paid Connecticut tobacco workers and, in the early twentieth century, worked vigorously to make Hartford, and all of Connecticut, a more just place for all. Yet for all intents and purposes, Mary Townsend Seymour has disappeared.

Attempts to discover details of her life on the Internet or in history books lead to mainly dead ends. The only public praise for her remarkable accomplishments as a founder of the Hartford chapter of the National Association for the Advancement of Colored People and advocate for both African American and women's rights is a small editorial in the September 11, 1952 *Hartford Courant*.

Just four paragraphs, the piece was written to mark the thirty-fifth anniversary of the Hartford NAACP and honor Mary, a woman "whose dedication to the freedom of the spirit was attested by her work":

> *Honor must go to this frail pioneer, this woman of culture whose mind and heart went out, not only to the oppressed people of her own race, but to subject people everywhere. It is good for today's generation to be reminded of the work that Mary T. Seymour started in Hartford 35 years ago.*

The only known photo of Mary Townsend Seymour. *Hartford Courant.*

In the ceremonies honoring her next week, we shall learn again that good citizenship and civic responsibility are not new virtues. For Mary Seymour and her husband, too, during his life, were active in everything that would promote the public good. "Conquering, holding, daring venturing as go the unknown ways, Pioneers, O pioneers!"

"My Name Is Mary Emma"

The youngest of seven children, Mary was born in Hartford on May 10, 1873, to Jacob and Emma Townsend, a cook and seamstress. Details of what happened to her parents are unknown, but Jacob's name disappears from Hartford records when Mary is seven, and it appears Emma moved to Windsor and then died when Mary was fifteen. What is known is that two months before her mother died in August 1888, Mary visited what was then Harford's Halls of Record at Trumbull and Pearl Streets and asked to see her birth record, which she apparently knew was incomplete, listing neither her first name nor her mother's maiden name. She told the clerk to add "Smith" to Emma's name and that her own name should be recorded as

As part of her work for civil and social justice, Mary helped form the Hartford chapter of the Circle for Negro War Relief, which helped African American soldiers like these marching in France during World War I. *U.S. Army Signal Corps/Library of Congress.*

Mary Emma Townsend Seymour. Noting "Name given by herself" in the far right-hand column, the clerk did as Mary instructed, and Mary walked out with a name that included the mother she loved and the family she was living with, the Seymours: Hartford African Americans headed by prominent Civil War veteran Lloyd Garrison Seymour, who was undoubtedly named after the famous white abolitionist.

Little is known about Mary during her young life. It's not until Mary turned eighteen and married Seymour family member Frederick Seymour in December 1891 that pieces of her life begin to come together. But even then, the details are vague.

In 1892, the two had a son whom they called Richie, but he died before he turned one. Mary and Frederick had no other children. Frederick worked for the U.S. Post Office. But instead of focusing solely on being a homemaker or working as a housekeeper or laundresses—then traditional jobs for African American women—Mary considered the world around her. Most of the African Americans in Hartford lived in poor housing and, when a serious crime occurred, were the first people police approached.

Between 1916 and 1917, she also watched the number of African Americans in Hartford more than double as thousands of families fled the Ku Klux Klan and the brazen lynchings taking place in the South. They wanted safety and believed the North would provide better jobs and better education. However, they weren't welcomed with open arms by all.

In the early twentieth century, even the most accepting communities had segregation laws, and Hartford was no different. Attitudes by many whites

ANTI-LYNCHING COMMITTEE

PHILIP G. PEABODY	MRS. LILLIAN A. ALEXANDER
MOORFIELD STOREY	W. E. B. DU BOIS
ARCHIBALD H. GRIMKE	MARY WHITE OVINGTON
JAMES WELDON JOHNSON	ARTHUR B. SPINGARN
WILLIAM ENGLISH WALLING	MRS. MINNIE L. BRADLEY
MRS. HELEN CURTIS	MRS. GENEVIEVE CANNON
MRS. MARY TOWNSEND SEYMOUR	

On the national level, Mary was a member of the NAACP's Anti-Lynching Committee, as noted in the NAACP's 1923 annual report. *Visual Materials from the National Association for the Advancement of Colored People Records/Library of Congress.*

and the infamous Jim Crow laws meant that even in this seemingly modern time, African Americans and whites did not mix in schools, libraries, movie theaters and other public places. Even in war, African Americans were found separately in what were known as Negro troops. Seeing these kinds of divides between not just blacks and whites but also men and women woke something in Mary. Scant records don't allow a comprehensive look at her political and social activism, but papers in the NAACP archives show that in January 1917, after attending an anti-lynching fundraiser, she and other attendees from Hartford discussed forming a local chapter.

Founded in 1909, the national NAACP was still a fledgling organization in 1917, but chapters were slowly forming in cities around the country. The national NAACP's focus at the time was discrimination and lynching and, at Mary's request, three of its national founders and leaders—James Weldon Johnson, Mary White Ovington and Dr. W.E.B. Du Bois—came to a meeting in October 1917 at Mary and Fred's house at 420 New Britain Avenue to discuss Connecticut's chapter. In addition to local African American leaders, three local white women active in the suffrage movement attended and committed to be charter members: Mary Bulkeley, Josephine Bennett and Katherine Beach Day.

With Hartford African American William Service Bell as president, Mary Seymour was responsible for both carrying out the chapter's day-to-day administrative work and, when Bell went off to Europe to fight in World War I, serving as its spokesperson.

A Fighter at Home

As much as World War I sparked the United States into action, it also sparked Mary. Living with outspoken veteran Lloyd Seymour during her teenage years, Mary must have been exposed to many of the issues that men and families faced during and after active war. Even if that wasn't the impetus, it was during these same years that Mary began her work with the NAACP that she also became active in several clubs formed to help Hartford African American World War I soldiers and their families, as well as southern families having a difficult time settling in the urban North.

She also joined the home service section of the American Red Cross and was horrified by the "wretched" living conditions of African American soldiers' families. Moved by the horror and sacrifices made by all involved in

Mary's signature.

war, she helped spearhead the creation of the Hartford chapter of the Circle for Negro War Relief, Inc., serving on its executive committee. She also joined the newly formed Colored Women's League of Hartford, intended to teach new residents the best way to cook, clean laundry, sew and perform other basic "domestic sciences."

In a letter to suffragist and Woman's Committee of the Connecticut State Council of Defense chairman Caroline Ruutz-Rees during this time, Mary talked passionately about the need for whites like Caroline to condemn lynchings, writing, "This thing of color prejudice has got to be reckoned with by those friends of your race who have the courage of their convictions to talk about it."

Clearly aware of the power of the press and the relationship between language and perception, Mary also took the *Hartford Courant* to task for publishing a letter to the editor that referred to African Americans as "darkys" and "niggahs," especially when referring to members of the United States' Negro Troops fighting overseas:

> *"Darky" and "niggah" are very objectionable to us. It would seem that white Americans, especially religious workers, would refrain from spreading American prejudice in France. These are inopportune times for the white press of this country to be offending its black millions. They are not satisfied with their lot in this democracy which is going forth to make the world safe for democracy. There are many parts of this country that are not decent places for them to live in—yet they are dying and going to die to "make the world a decent place to live in." They have more to forget and forgive than any racial group beneath the Stars and Stripes.*
>
> *Under such circumstances, the Caucasian newspaper that sows this sort of discord and dissension among the brave and badly needed black fighters of America at this time is doing a wicked, seditious, unpatriotic thing. We want to inform these dailies that colored citizens do not enjoy being made fun of. They would do not only a welcome but a wide thing to let their*

*negrophobe readers forego for a while the pleasure of being amused at the
expense of our people—for the sake of winning the war.*

Accompanying Mary's letter in the July 2, 1918 *Courant* was an editor's
note explaining that while "*The Courant* readily prints this letter...it does not
hesitate to declare that the writer is too sensitive. [The letter Mary responded
to], as we read it, did not make fun of the negro soldiers. It did quote their
peculiar dialect." They offered something of an apology at the end: "If the
word darky offends colored people, as it may, they can be assured that, if it
appears again in *The Courant*, that it will be by accident and against the rules
of the office."

Labor and Women's Issues

Mary's work with the Red Cross led her into the Connecticut River Valley's
tobacco fields, where she discovered that workers, particularly African
American women, were spending backbreaking hours in the warehouses
but being cheated out of their daily wages. Mary decided to investigate
by changing into work clothes and spending a day hand-stripping and
stemming tobacco herself. The NAACP journal the *Crisis* wrote an article
about her findings:

> *Payment was made in such a fashion that no one could tell how much
> she could make a week. One woman, a widow of a soldier with four
> children, made $3.90; another $1.62; another as low as 40 cents. They
> were worked irregularly and cheated in many little ways. The weighing
> was often unfair, the foreman taking advantage of the fact that most of
> his employees could not read the scales. But those who could read them
> were unable to get proper pay for their work, the foremen either making all
> manner of fun of the one who protested, successfully jollying her, or driving
> her to anger that she left. Then, again, the tobacco would be weighed dry
> when the proper price was for tobacco weighed wet. It was evident to Mrs.
> Seymour as she worked by the side of these newcomers, wholly unversed in
> their tasks, that they needed the protection of organization.*

Mary urged the female workers to organize a union and fight for their
rights. It was a daring move, as most of the local African American ministers

spoke against unions in their sermons. However, with the help of fellow suffragist and Hartford NAACP member Josephine Bennett, Mary was able to get sixty workers to sign on.

But as it was in so much of America, Connecticut's tobacco region was divided by racism and that, coupled with unfair labor practices, caused the union to soon fall apart. Mary insisted that a day would come when African American and white workers would form an alliance and work side by side to advance their common interests. She believed the same equality could be achieved between women and men and, in 1920, ran for office in the Connecticut General Assembly as a member of the Farmer-Labor Party that had formed two years earlier.

Like most Farmer-Labor candidates that year, Mary lost the election. But her efforts earned her a place in history books as the first African American woman in the nation to run for a state-level office.

Leading efforts to establish literacy classes to teach Hartford African Americans how to read and write, Mary remained active in the NAACP for several years, working both locally and as a member of the national

Mary rests in a hard-to-find plot toward the back of Hartford's Old North Cemetery on Main Street. Note that the year of her death was never added to her gravestone.

NAACP's Anti-Lynching Committee. According to the NAACP's 1923 annual report, her committee's work the previous year led to "encouraging results," including the number of known lynchings in the United States decreasing from sixty-one to twenty-eight.

Even after she officially retired from the Hartford NAACP executive board in late 1926, Mary remained active behind the scenes, advising the organization's new and emerging leaders and helping Hartford African Americans find jobs within the white community. Of the NAACP, she said, "The Association is so dear to me."

Mary died on January 12, 1957, after a long illness. She was eighty-three. In 1998, the nonprofit My Sister's Place named its new women's shelter on North Main Street the Mary Seymour Place in her honor.

Five years before, in the *Hartford Courant* editorial celebrating the Hartford NAACP's thirty-fifth anniversary, editors reminded readers, "Nearly all human progress is the work of a few dedicated persons." Even in her sadly unkempt grave, Mary can rest easy knowing she was one of those few.

Chapter 8

BEATRICE FOX AUERBACH

BUSINESS LEADER AND PHILANTHROPIST: 1887–1968

B eatrice Fox Auerbach's innovative sales practices and pioneering labor reforms led to Hartford's G. Fox & Company becoming not just the largest department store in Connecticut but also the largest privately held department store in the United States. Emphasizing the importance of overall excellence and quality customer service, her forward-thinking enhancements included free delivery, a toll-free telephone sales department and automated billing—all brand-new concepts at the time. As dedicated to her staff as to her customers, Beatrice believed in the power of loyalty and created what then were unheard-of employee benefits, such as company-sponsored retirement plans, paid vacations, a forty-hour work week, an in-store hospital and a cafeteria that sold meals at cost.

For Linda Glickstein of Philadelphia, however, Beatrice was Granny:

> *Granny was a great business woman. She was dignified. Astute. But she was also a warm woman who always put her family first and believed that all people, no matter what their color or religion, should be treated the same. The benefits she offered her employees, and the way she treated them, made them fiercely loyal. She didn't just spend time with executive employees. She believed every single worker had something to give. That was a big lesson I took from her: You can learn from everyone.*

Beatrice Fox Auerbach and her sister Fanny at the unveiling of a portrait of their father, Moses Fox. *Connecticut Historical Society.*

Unexpected Calling

Born in Hartford on July 7, 1887, Beatrice was the oldest of Moses and Theresa Stern Fox's two daughters. Forty years earlier, her grandfather Gerson Fox founded G. Fox on Main Street. By the time Beatrice was born, her father, Moses, had already been working there for more than twenty years. He took over as president in 1880 when Gerson died.

As a girl, Beatrice attended several schools, traveled widely and worked part time as a G. Fox sales clerk, but she did not go to college. In 1911, she married George Auerbach, whose family owned the F. Auerbach & Brother department store in Salt Lake City. As newlyweds, they lived in Utah. But when G. Fox burned down in January 1917, George brought Beatrice home to Hartford with plans that he would become secretary and treasurer of a new and expanded G. Fox and help Moses rebuild.

Back with her family, Beatrice was interested in G. Fox and helped where needed, but her daughters, Georgette and Dorothy, were her primary focus. The four Auerbachs lived in a large, brick Gothic- and Tudor-style home on

Beatrice and George's official engagement photo. *Connecticut Historical Society.*

Prospect Avenue known for its connecting twin gables. But when George died suddenly in 1927, Beatrice went back to working at G. Fox part time, overseeing day-to-day operations on what she thought was going to be a temporary basis. But to her surprise, she found herself "fascinated and stayed."

When her father died in 1938, she assumed the role of president of G. Fox, a position she held for twenty-seven years. Rena Koopman of Massachusetts often thinks about her grandmother's accomplishments, saying, "Growing up, she wasn't raised or trained to take over the family business. But when she did, she didn't just run her business well, she ran it in a way that no one had ever run a business before. Repeatedly, she bucked popular wisdom and ideas, and instead followed her own beliefs. She was an extraordinary woman ahead of her time and her decisions raised the standards for everyone."

One of the first changes Beatrice made to G. Fox was to the building itself. She refined the inside, adding Art Deco details and, above the Main Street entrance, installing what became the store's signature Art Deco marquee.

A vintage postcard of the G. Fox building in Hartford.

Other physical changes that occurred during her tenure included a nine-story retail addition to the rear Market Street side, a new major warehouse and a multilevel parking garage built in the 1960s. Adamantly against branch stores that she believed detracted from the appeal of a flagship store, Beatrice bucked what appeared to be a growing national trend and, instead of opening satellites, turned part of the Toy Department on the eleventh floor into a telephone order facility. Included were first-of-its-kind direct phone lines that allowed Connecticut, Massachusetts and Rhode Island shoppers to call toll free.

The store itself was known for its lively and one-of-a-kind displays, which included a talking myna bird on the fifth floor. In the Home Department, furnishings for kitchens, living rooms and bedrooms were set up like actual rooms—something no store had done before. There were also two restaurants on the second floor that sometimes hosted fashion shows. "All of this made going to G. Fox a real experience," Rena added.

Champion for Workplace Reform

The changes and experiences Beatrice is best known for, however, are those that involve the groundbreaking employee benefits and practices she instituted. Unheard-of policies that allowed for paid vacations, granted interest-free loans for personal emergencies, established an in-store hospital and offered school scholarships resulted in G. Fox becoming a national leader in workforce reform. For Beatrice, it also resulted in steadfastly loyal employees who looked forward to not just the holiday bonuses that inevitably came but also the personal letter from Beatrice that announced them, like this one from November 1960:

> *My own Thanks-giving embraces each and every one of you, for your loyalty to G. Fox & Company, for the strength I find in knowing that your support and striving will speed our growth in the days ahead. This year has been marked by increased expenses of operations and customer services with narrow rewards, yet G. Fox & Company, through me, wishes to express tangible recognition of your devoted work.*

Linda also remembers talking with Granny Beatrice about why the store was closed on Sundays and Mondays. She recalled, "I'm pretty sure

GO-GETTER

PUBLISHED WEEKLY BY AND FOR THE EMPLOYEES OF G. FOX AND CO.

Volume XXVII Number 44 November 22, 1960

Hartford, Connecticut

G.FOX*CO.
HARTFORD · CONNECTICUT

Serving Connecticut since 1847

OFFICE OF THE PRESIDENT

NOVEMBER 22, 1960

DEAR ASSOCIATES:

LET US JOIN HEARTS IN GRATEFULNESS ON THIS THANKSGIVING DAY FOR OUR FREEDOMS AS AMERICANS!

MY OWN THANKS-GIVING EMBRACES EACH AND EVERY ONE OF YOU, FOR YOUR LOYALTY TO G. FOX & COMPANY, FOR THE STRENGTH I FIND IN KNOWING THAT YOUR SUPPORT AND STRIVING WILL SPEED OUR GROWTH IN THE DAYS AHEAD.

THIS YEAR HAS BEEN MARKED BY INCREASED EXPENSES OF OPERATION AND CUSTOMER SERVICES WITH NARROWED REWARDS, YET G. FOX COMPANY, THROUGH ME, WISHES TO EXPRESS TANGIBLE RECOGNITION OF YOUR DEVOTED WORK, DECLARING THE 1960 BONUS ACCORDING TO THE TABLE ON THE REVERSE SIDE OF THIS GO-GETTER.

WITH IT GOES MY WARMEST THANKSGIVING WISHES TO YOU AND YOUR FAMILY, AS YOU CELEBRATE THE HOLIDAY TOGETHER.

CORDIALLY,

Beatrice Fox Auerbach

BEATRICE FOX AUERBACH

Many former G. Fox employees have commented on the small but personal ways Beatrice reached out and made them feel like family.

Connecticut blue laws mandated that all stores be closed on Sundays. But Granny kept the store closed on Mondays because she felt it was important that employees have time each week to spend with their families, which a five-day work week ensured."

Sunday was the big family day for the Auerbachs, which when Linda and Rena were young included Beatrice's daughters, son-in-laws and twelve grandchildren. To ensure that Beatrice got to spend time and really talk with each one of them, she hosted two meals on Sundays: a lunch for her and her grandchildren only, and then an evening dinner with the adults. As Linda remembers it, the menu was much the same each week: for the kids, a shrimp cocktail appetizer, followed by meat, potatoes and a vegetable. For Beatrice, scrambled eggs and bacon. Linda recalled:

> *She liked to sleep late on Sundays, so she was still on breakfast when we arrived. But it was a very formal affair with good china, Sterling silverware, cloth napkins, silver salt and pepper shakers. Sometimes if we got there early, the girls could sit with her in her dressing room as she did her hair and put on her face creams and makeup. It was all very ritualized but very wonderful. Because when we grandchildren were there, Granny made us feel like nothing was important but us.*

Employees tended to feel the same way, which was proven each year when Beatrice presented Moses Fox Club awards to those who had attained twenty-five and fifty years of service. Customers also were loyal—and they had good reason to be. Personal shoppers, free home delivery and an automated billing system were among the services G. Fox provided long before they became standard elsewhere. Guided by Moses's belief and the G. Fox motto of "Honesty, Courtesy and Service," Beatrice also expected as much of her employees as she expected of herself. Managers were required to be on the floor at all times on Saturdays; salespersons were expected to be able to answer questions about every item; and at all times, departments had to be clean and orderly, with no merchandise out of stock or not offered in a wide variety of colors, sizes, styles and prices.

Beatrice was also known for making daily, white-gloved sweeps of the sales counters and making a point of knowing the name of every employee and as many customers as possible. "My grandmother didn't just remember her employees' names, but their children's and sometimes even their grandchildren's names," Rena remembered. "Whether you were the gardener or Eleanor Roosevelt, if you were interesting, she wanted to talk to you. And really, she thought everyone was interesting."

She also thought race should not determine what job you held and, in 1942, G. Fox became the first store in the United States to put African Americans into visible sales and management positions.

Community Servant

As much as Beatrice gave to her store, employees and customers, she also gave to the community. Eager to help others attain similar success, she established and funded the Service Bureau for Women's Organizations to teach members of women's groups how to conduct meetings, coordinate activities and effectively lobby. Interested also in helping other women succeed in retail, she collaborated with Connecticut College for Women (now Connecticut College) to establish a retail program that used her store as a laboratory for students to perform hands-on learning.

Through the Beatrice Fox Auerbach Foundation, she gave generous gifts to many organizations, including New York's Mount Sinai Hospital and the Hebrew Home for the Aged. A patron of the arts, she endowed the Hartford Symphony Orchestra's director's chair, paid for the acquisition of ten thousand books for the Wadsworth Atheneum library and funded scholarships at Saint Joseph College, Wesleyan University, the Hartford Conservatory of Music, the University of Hartford and the University of Connecticut. She also endowed an economics professorship at Trinity College and gave to many other cultural, medical and educational institutes throughout Hartford and Connecticut.

In July 1944, when the Ringling Brothers and Barnum & Bailey Circus tent burned down during an afternoon performance and injured seven hundred people in one of the worst fire disasters in U.S. history, Beatrice sent four nurses from G. Fox's employee hospital to assist on the site, instructed her delivery drivers and vans to help shuttle as many patients and people who needed rides and donated linens and pajamas to local hospitals.

Beatrice fostered that same spirit of giving in her grandchildren, Rena said:

As part of our Sunday lunches, we were expected to put however many coins we had in our pockets into a special container. It could be a nickel, a quarter,

Beatrice's signature.

First Lady Eleanor Roosevelt was one of Beatrice's dear friends. *Connecticut Historical Society.*

a dollar—whatever we wanted. We'd do that for one year, and then take it out and count it. Beatrice would match whatever money was in there, and we'd donate it to a charity. The lesson was that little bits add up.

Similarly, when we were done with lunch and left the table, she expected us to go into the kitchen and thank every person who was involved in preparing and serving our meal. She believed so strongly in appreciating and respecting the people who help and support you.

In 1947, G. Fox celebrated its 100th anniversary, which Beatrice marked with a yearlong Centennial Celebration that included newspaper advertisements, commemorative books, special window displays and a day when all deliveries were made by helicopter. That same year, Beatrice was awarded with what was then the highest award in retailing, the Tobé Award for Distinguished Contribution to American Retailing. In her acceptance speech, Beatrice said:

[This] *is one of those rare experiences in a lifetime that one cherishes and remembers. I accept it proudly, aware of the high standards by which its recipients are chosen. Yet my pride is tempered with humility. Whatever I may have done to be named for this distinction is not mine alone. It is but part of a heritage from the past, a partnership with the present, and a trusteeship for the future...The store was founded by my grandfather and for fifty-eight years directed by my father. From them, and from the tradition of New England, I—as the third generation—learned the values of steadfast principles in life and in work...I know that no one's work is done alone. It is extended on every front by the creative talents and devoted efforts of one's associates—from the highest to the humblest. It is they who carry on the activities of an institution day by day and their energies, fused with one's own, forge an institutional character as distinctive as human character.*

At the peak of the store's success, Beatrice oversaw four thousand staff members and a fleet of 147 trucks that delivered as many as 2 million packages each year. In 1965 at age seventy-eight, Beatrice sold the company to May Department Stores for a reported $40 million and remained president until shortly before her death in 1968.

G. Fox closed permanently in 1992. But the building—complete with its Art Deco marquee—is still a Hartford landmark. Part of it is home to Capital Community College, a use of which Beatrice would almost definitely approve.

"My grandmother felt that every day, there were lessons to be learned. Everything was a teachable moment for her," remembered Rena Koopman. "She also talked about trusting your gut. You can change your original opinion, she believed, but it was important to tune in to your instincts. She wasn't the usual grandmother in the kitchen baking cookies. She was so much more. It was the biggest treat in the world to have her for a grandmother." Remarkable, indeed.

Chapter 9

RACHEL TAYLOR MILTON

FOUNDER OF GREATER HARTFORD'S
URBAN LEAGUE: 1901–1995

The first African American woman to graduate from the Hartford Seminary School of Religious Education, Rachel Taylor Milton's dream to work as a Christian missionary was realized not in Africa, as she imagined, but in her own backyard. Inspired by her faith and motivated by the belief that every person must learn to recognize the "human dignity of another," Rachel in the midst of the often volatile racial divides of the 1960s helped found and then ensure the future of the Urban League of Greater Hartford. An affiliate of the national Urban League, this nonprofit located on Hartford's Woodland Street is today one of the largest direct social service agencies in New England. Although the types of services the agency offers have changed, its mission is the same as when Rachel helped open its doors: empowering disadvantaged African Americans with the educational, employment and economic training they need to become their best selves and live their best lives.

"The civil and human rights movements that Rachel worked so hard to advance were supposed to be the start of an era of change, but I'm afraid nobody's work is done," said current Hartford Urban League president and CEO Adrienne Cochrane. "The reality is that the more things change, the more things stay the same, because problems like poverty and violence? They still very much exist. Rachel and those she worked with helped us find our collective voices, but we have to continue to move forward the work they began."

In 1970, Rachel told *Hartford Times* staff writer Ron Thody how that beginning included her and co-founders Marion Hepburn Grant, Dr.

A young Rachel at far left in roughly 1910. *Maureen Hicks/Taylor family.*

James S. Peters II, Judge Norris O'Neill and Olcott Smith literally "crying the League into existence," pleading to anyone who'd listen for the desks, mimeograph machine, chairs and typewriters needed to set up the organization's first office.

It was work that perhaps, in many ways, Rachel was born to do: "[My] parents taught us that we were human beings and you had worth because you were a human being," she told her great-niece Patricia Anderson of Hartford in 1986. "We must do things that are related to the needs of people…We need to change the cycle of apathy into a cycle of action."

A Call to Faith

Born in Hartford on May 19, 1901, Rachel was one of ten children of John Taylor, a builder, and his wife, Mary, a seamstress who, as Rachel once described it, worked in Virginia in "the big house." The two moved to Hartford, where Rachel and her brother and sisters would attend Hartford schools. Her father helped found Hartford's Union Baptist Church, and there her faith emerged.

At the shore. *Patricia Anderson/Taylor family.*

After graduating from the Hartford Seminary in 1923, she went on to attend the University of Pittsburgh, the New York School of Social Work and the University of Chicago, as well as took part in Swarthmore College's First Institute on Race Relations. Her professional career included serving as executive director of YWCAs in Pittsburgh, Omaha, Nashville and Chicago; associate dean of women at Nashville's Fisk University; and director of the Chicago Housing Authority's first interracial senior citizens' center.

After marrying Baptist pastor Charles Milton, she returned to Hartford to work for the Connecticut Bureau for Vocational Rehabilitation, where she witnessed a paradox, she said. How, she wondered, could there be such divisiveness and poverty in such a wealthy city? A letter she wrote to the *Hartford Courant* in 1969 shows that she, at least in part, blamed the media:

> *It's about time for the press to quit using its pages to dramatize the conflicts…of the Negro community and communicate with positiveness the directions for better living…Greed for money and power keep our city from being truly an American city. We do not all think alike, nor do we all behave alike…In each man is God, and what a difference it would make if we could but see his image in all people. I am like many readers, tired of hearing about the conflict, and thirsting to hear of the change!*

Her return to Hartford brought her back to Union Baptist Church. There, she sang in the chancel choir and chaired the committee to have it listed on the National Register of Historic Places for its leaders' roles in the early civil rights movement, including the Reverend John Jackson's work to help establish the Connecticut Inter-Racial Commission, which evolved into the Commission on Human Rights and Opportunities.

This kind of community involvement and outreach through her job led Rachel to the meeting where the idea for a Hartford chapter of the

Rachel's signature.

Urban League came about. There, the six people talking about the need for African Americans to have better housing, jobs and neighborhoods decided to take the first step toward achieving these goals by each putting $5 into an envelope. In less than five years, with Rachel as one of the handful leading the efforts, that $30 (plus grants, corporate gifts from companies like the Travelers and countless individual donations) morphed into the $90,000 needed for the league to open its doors. As Rachel told the *Hartford Times*, "We just kept getting there by pennies...[At first] we were just inching along. It was fortunate for us that we had the kind of people who stuck together."

Leading the League

Then Secretary of State Ella Grasso and activist and author Marion Hepburn Grant (sister of actress Katharine Hepburn) were among those who sat with Rachel on the Urban League's first board of directors. Andrea Brown Seldon, whose father, Dr. William J. Brown, was hired to serve as the league's first president and CEO, remembers Rachel as a "determined powerhouse who always wanted more":

> *Between African Americans and whites, Rachel wanted parity in education, parity in housing, parity in employment, parity in everything. I was eleven or twelve when I met her for the first time, and she had such a laugh. I know that sounds very general, but she had this bright, bold laugh that was infectious and that made you pay attention to what she was going to say after she was done. And she was determined. Rachel was saying, "Yes we can" long before President Obama. She wanted equality.*

It's impossible to say exactly what aspects of inequality upset or angered Rachel most. Any papers she might have left behind are gone or buried so deep in boxes of family or Urban League archives that they can't be easily found. But it's possible that the thoughts that Patricia Anderson wrote down after interviewing her great-aunt Rachel shed some light.

Patricia was a student at Yale Divinity School in 1986, taking a class in Afro-American Critical Thought, when she sat down with Aunt Rae, who, at the time, was eighty-seven and, according to Patricia's report, "a handsome woman with brown skin devoid of any aging lines. She speaks deliberately in her deep voice. Her memory is sharp."

Black Women of Connecticut: Achievements Against the Odds

Rachel was among those featured in *Black Women of Connecticut: Achievements Against the Odds*, published in 1984 by the Connecticut Historical Society.

Most of what Patricia writes about Rachel has to do with situations Rachel encountered with white staff when she worked for the YWCA in Pennsylvania and Nashville. But within the text, Patricia shares some of her own experiences growing up in Hartford as an African American in the 1940s and '50s:

As a young child, I thought that Jim Crow was an actual human being. Gradually I learned that Jim Crow lived through institutions and persons and is morally wrong. Grandpa, however, was not naïve enough to believe that racial tension did not exist in the North... [At the dinner table] *I heard family stories. An extremely talented uncle could not play baseball in the major leagues because society said that he was born too soon. This all-state high school star, who was scouted by the majors, was not approached after it was realized he was of color. He is still very bitter about the viciousness of his experience with racial discrimination.*

My grandmother loved to tell the story of the incident when she was instructed to sit downstairs in the movie theater in Hartford, but that her two children would have to sit upstairs. Grandma was fair-skinned, but her son and daughter were brown. They all sat downstairs. She was feisty and refused the edict of the management.

I never internalized the reality of slave life in the North. Our social studies books and history school books portrayed African slaves as less than human, working on Southern plantations. The North was not mentioned. Since then, I have learned that Connecticut was the last Northern state to give up slavery, and reluctantly at that.

It's almost possible to imagine Rachel nodding knowingly as her niece shared these stories. In 1964, shortly before Rachel and her fellow advocates opened the Urban League, Congress passed the Civil Rights Act of 1964 that prohibited discrimination on the basis of race, color, religion, sex or national origin. It was groundbreaking legislation meant to change the attitudes and practices of a nation. But the truth was that things in Hartford and elsewhere weren't immediately all that different than they had been in the days, weeks, months or years before, despite what the potentially far-reaching legislation had promised.

U.S. Supreme Court decisions like *Brown v. the Board of Education* in 1954 that deemed that segregation in education was unconstitutional had brought new and renewed enthusiasm to the civil rights cause both locally and throughout the nation. Dr. Martin Luther King Jr. also came to Hartford in 1959, making an impassioned plea for an end to racism in the United States. Many believe it was an early version of his famous "I Have a Dream"

Rachel in the 1960s with fellow Hartford Urban League co-founder Marion Hepburn Grant and William Brown, the agency's first executive director. *Urban League.*

speech, which he would deliver four years later on the steps of the Lincoln Memorial in Washington, D.C.

Yet despite pleas and potential, African Americans in Hartford—like those around the country—were still being denied jobs and educational opportunities because of their color. Poverty and discrimination among African Americans were norms, rather than exceptions, and the city, like too many others, was racially divided.

But Rachel had the gift of being able to draw people together, Andrea Brown Seldon remembered. "She was such a role model for young women. She and my father would always tell me, 'The sky's the limit. You can do whatever you want.'"

Committed to the Community

Rachel gave time and energy to agencies and organizations throughout Hartford. In addition to helping establish the Urban League, she founded the Junior Council of the National Council of Negro Women, was a charter member of the National Business and Professional Women's Association's Hartford chapter and was a member of the Mayor's Committee on Minority Problems, the Regional Council, Greater Hartford Community Colleges, the Women's Auxiliary of the Hartford Symphony Orchestra, Interdenominational Ministers' Wives Alliance, National Association for the Advancement of Colored Persons and the Harriet Beecher Stowe Foundation.

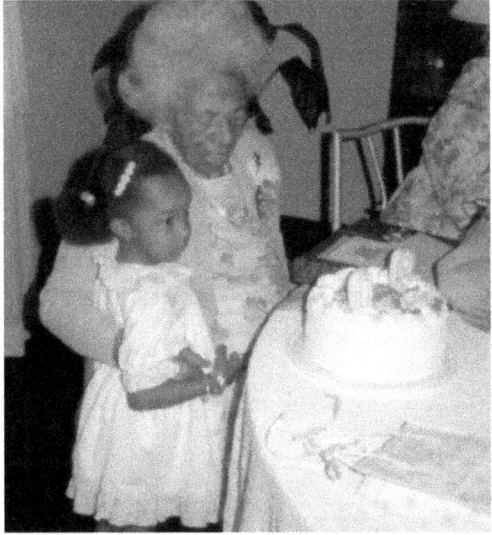

At her ninetieth birthday party with great-niece Kyle Boatright. *Rachel King/Taylor family.*

Over the years, she received numerous awards, including a "Citation of Merit" from the Hartford Seminary Foundation. The certificate in part reads: "In times of discordant polarization in our society, her charismatic gifts and skills have served the cause of mediation and reconciliation between Black and White, between regional life styles, between the generations, between theory and practice, and between women and men."

Rachel died on July 4, 1995, in a nursing home just outside Hartford. She was ninety-four, but even shortly before her death was still telling stories. One of her favorites was about singing—something she was extremely good at—and the life lesson she learned through song.

According to her recounting to the *Hartford Times*, when she was a student at Fisk University, she sought out a well-known voice teacher—a white woman—for lessons. The teacher at first looked at Rachel strangely but instructed her to sing several songs. Then, the teacher asked Rachel to sit down:

> [She told me] *she could not teach me because if white girls knew she was teaching a colored person, they would stop coming to her studio. I felt deeply hurt. But she thought I had a good voice and asked if she could come to me and teach me. I went home and sort of dismissed the idea. I suppose my*

pride was hurt. That's what really bothered me. Then a friend said if the teacher was willing to go halfway, I should be willing to go halfway, too.

Compromise and effort became two of the many positive qualities Rachel was known for, though never would she back away from her beliefs. Her remarkable sense of hope that change would come for anyone willing to work hard and believe is still what transforms lives and communities today.

Chapter 10

HILDA CROSBY STANDISH

MEDICAL DIRECTOR OF CONNECTICUT'S FIRST BIRTH CONTROL CLINIC: 1902–2005

Medical director of Connecticut's first birth control clinic at a time when contraceptive distribution and use was illegal, Hilda Crosby Standish, MD, was a pioneer in the field of sex education and family planning who changed—and in several instances saved—the lives of generations of women.

"The courage she showed speaking up and advocating for women to have this basic right to control their bodies and have access to preventive healthcare was truly remarkable, and her legacy lives on today," said Planned Parenthood of Southern New England CEO and executive director Judy Tabar, who met Hilda when she was ninety-five and still acting as a consultant for the women's health organization.

Thirty years after this 1952 photo was taken, Planned Parenthood of Connecticut renamed its West Hartford site the Hilda Crosby Standish, MD, Clinic. *Standish family*

"I remember an afternoon when Hilda was close to one hundred, and she and I had plans for lunch. I watched her drive into the West Hartford clinic parking lot, leap out of the car and then go inside to speak to staff, because she was always interested in saying hello and hearing how things were going."

Training and Traveling

A young Hilda, 1915. *Standish family.*

The middle daughter of Albert and Julia Case Crosby, Hilda was born in 1902 on Sergeant Street in Hartford but soon moved with her family to the second floor of a duplex on Vine Street. In a November 2002 interview with Julie Bazenas from the Connecticut Women's Hall of Fame, Hilda explained how as a grade school student, she'd wake up her friend Mildred in the apartment below. She said, "I would take a long string, and on the end of it I would tie a nail, and swing it out and let it come in until it hit Mildred's window... She would wake up, and then we would go to Keeney Park and pick up chestnuts before school. We got quite full bags."

Hilda said she knew at an early age that she wanted to spend her life helping others. As she stated in a 1998 speech: "I had been very anxious since childhood, and hearing the minister of our First Baptist Church preach on foreign missions, I had always had the feeling I'd like to make my life worthwhile. I wanted to try medicine." While a student at Hartford Public High School, she also volunteered at local hospitals.

Neither of her parents attended college, and her father was especially insistent that his three daughters go. After considering schools in New York and Connecticut, Hilda decided on Wellesley College in Massachusetts, where she pursued a degree in zoology.

Four years at Cornell Medical College followed, along with an internship at Philadelphia General Hospital, a residency in obstetrics at the St. Louis Maternity Hospital and additional training and work at New York's Bellevue Hospital. In 1997, apparently at the request of the Cornell Medical College alumni office, Hilda shared her reasons for choosing Cornell, as well as some of her experiences there:

> *Which medical school? Yale, closest to my home in Hartford, admitted only two to three women per year, and Harvard allowed no women to darken its sacred doorstep. In the spring of 1924 at an interview with Dean Niles at Cornell, I asked: "May I enter in the fall if I pass a summer course in organic chemistry?"*
>
> *Bless him. He said yes. And I did.*
>
> *The Medical School was at 28th Street and First Avenue, a single building with housing, labs, lecture hall and adjacent [operating rooms]. We numbered 67, 11 of whom were women…And let me tell you, never throughout my student years at Cornell or later during my intern or residency appointments did I experience any treatment different from that of the men. We were all doctors.*
>
> *There were no dorms in those days. I lived in a nearby girls' club freshman year, and for the next three with four other Cornell women rented a small third-floor apartment on East 19th Street, just off First Avenue. Daytime or evening, in groups or alone, in those days it was safe to walk in the streets or ride the subways.*
>
> *We left Cornell in 1928, grateful for the privilege of training under such remarkable teachers.*

In 1932, Hilda was offered and accepted an appointment to serve as an assistant professor of obstetrics at the Women's Christian Medical College and Margaret Williamson Hospital in Shanghai, China. There, she performed what many believe was the first blood transfusion in the country. Hilda also wrote about this experience:

> *Truly wanting to serve where most needed, by happy chance I heard of an opening in a 200-bed hospital…with 100 of those beds for obstetricians and a chance to teach in English in their small medical college for Chinese women. What an experience! Living in the Chinese section of the city,*

While in China, Hilda performed what many believe was the first blood transfusion in the country. *Standish family.*

teaching, introducing a simple but adequate method of blood transfusion, frequent visits to inland villages on weekends. And, at the end, I spent three months among the treasures of Peking, when one still saw the old walls, dirt roads and camel train. The trip was three weeks by ship.

Back to Hartford

A letter from her father saying that both her mother and younger sister were ill forced Hilda to come home to Connecticut after just two years in China. Her plan was to eventually return, but the Japanese invasion of Shanghai the following year made it impossible. It also soon became clear that her medical expertise and practical, no-nonsense approach to women's health were needed at home.

In 1935, she was recruited by fellow Hartford resident and social reformer Katharine Martha Houghton Hepburn (mother of actress Katharine Hepburn) to serve as medical director of the Maternal Health Center at 100 Retreat Avenue in Hartford. The facility was established by Hepburn's Connecticut Birth Control League (which eventually evolved into Planned Parenthood), but the move was a risky one.

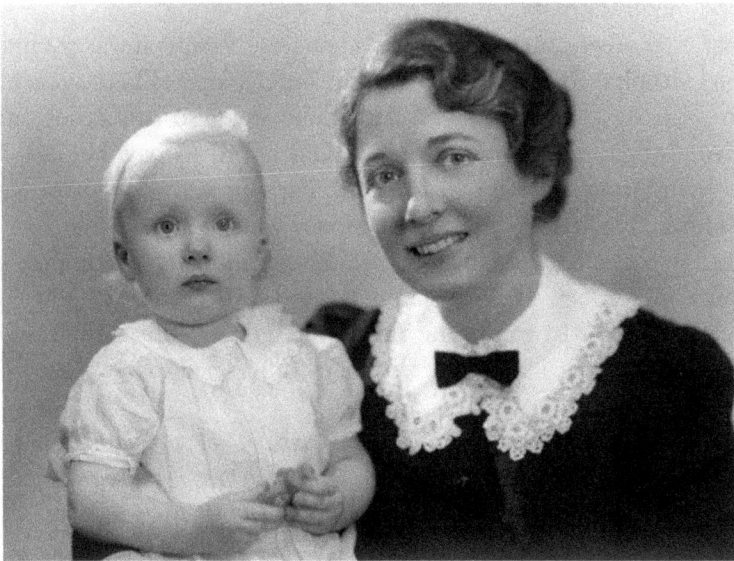

With her daughter Nancy. *Standish family.*

As late as 1961, laws in several states, including Connecticut, made the distribution and even the use of contraceptives a criminal offense. It wasn't until 1965 that the ban was decreed unconstitutional by the landmark U.S. Supreme Court case *Griswold v. Connecticut*, which was sparked by Hartford-born civil rights activist Estelle Griswold, executive director of the Planned Parenthood in New Haven and Hilda's former high school classmate.

During Hilda's tenure at the Maternal Health Center, the diaphragms and other contraceptives she quietly gave to patients in examination rooms were in direct violation of the Comstock Law. Named after Connecticut-born politician Anthony Comstock who proposed it, the law enacted in 1879 stated that "any person who uses any drug, medicinal article or instrument for the purposes of preventing conception shall be fined not less than forty dollars or imprisoned not less than sixty days." Also, "any person who assists, abets, counsels, causes, hires or commands another to commit any offense may be prosecuted and punished as if he were the principle offender."

Often approached by the media for commentary, Hilda told reporters more than once that she believed the Comstock Law was "stupid and outmoded" and downplayed the personal risk she took by violating the law. Many of the more than three thousand women she saw at the clinic were mothers of as many as twelve or fourteen children and desperate for diaphragms, condoms or whatever other means of birth control Hilda or her colleagues could provide. She said, "None of us felt like pioneers. This was just good medical practice."

Apparently other physicians felt the same way, because it was common for Hartford Hospital doctors to stop by the clinic, asking Hilda to teach them how to properly fit a diaphragm. The clinic was also run almost entirely off private donations, as few women could afford to pay. Hilda told the Connecticut Women's Hall of Fame, "Trying to raise five or six or eight or nine children…Where do you get the money when you have that?"

But despite active lobbing by healthcare providers, women's rights advocates and others, state legislators refused to overturn the edict. Hilda testified in Hartford against the law several times. But until *Griswold v. Connecticut*, her efforts, like those of so many others, led to few gains:

For years I continued to work for the overturn of the archaic Comstock Law, but due to constant Catholic opposition, this was not achieved until 1965, when the Supreme Court declared the law illegal due to the invasion of privacy. In the late '30s at the request of friends, I had begun to show films and answer questions to girls and boys separately on changes at the

The Standish family, 1949. *Standish family.*

time of adolescence. This expanded quickly to discussions with groups of premarital couples and lectures to parents that helped, I hope, in answering questions about sex. Religious opposition continued to make the going rough at times, but improved greatly as the years went on.

The clinic stayed open for five years but was forced to close in 1940 after the arrests of two doctors and a nurse at the Connecticut Birth Control League's Waterbury clinic site. By this time, Hilda had been married for four years to dermatologist Myles Standish and had begun to start a family. She considered opening a private practice but instead decide to devote her time to raising her five children and speaking about human development, sex education and family planning to schools, churches and, for the most part, anyone who'd listen. Said her son Rick Standish:

At the time, no one else was talking about this stuff, though I have to say that I only heard her speak once or twice myself. I mean, kids are always a little embarrassed about their parents, so imagine what it was like to have your mom being the one telling people you know all about sex. But even though I didn't want to hear her speak, others sure did. She was in demand, and I think a lot of it had to do with how she presented the topic. She was very straightforward, very authentic and matter-of-fact. And she was as tough as she was loving, which was important when protestors showed up at one of her talks.

Impact and Influence

Hilda spent the majority of her professional life traveling and speaking about sexuality and preventive sex—a practice that continued even after she retired in 1962 and up until she was at least one hundred. Rick recalled, "There really was no stopping her." In Hilda's own words, as a sex educator, she gave parents words "that they could use if they wanted to explain parts of the body and how things worked" to their children. Before school talks, students needed to hand in notes giving their parents' written permission to attend small group sessions with Hilda about how babies are born and how devices like diaphragms can help prevent pregnancy from occurring.

During World War II, she also served on Hartford's Civil Defense Force and volunteered in the Department of Anesthesia at Hartford Hospital. When the Planned Parenthood League of Connecticut emerged in 1961, she aligned herself with the organization and its efforts to legalize birth control, which, thanks in no small part to her efforts, occurred on June 7, 1964.

She also served as a member of West Hartford's School Health Advisory Council. To honor her contributions and dedication to the field, Planned Parenthood of Connecticut in 1993 renamed the West Hartford clinic the Hilda Crosby Standish, MD Clinic. Her other honors include a Doctor of Humane Letters from the University of Hartford and Wellesley's Alumnae Achievement Award. At the Wellesley award presentation ceremony, Hilda shared a story about a recent phone call:

I picked up the phone and the voice said, "Dr. Hilda? I want to throw my arms around you. You saved my life."

"But who's this?" I asked. "What do you mean?"

Her words gushed out, and she said to me, "I am eighty-six. I am a Catholic. I grew up in a family of fourteen. I never went to school, never sat inside a classroom. I had to help my mother with the children, cook, sew, wash and later go to work. I learned to read from newspapers. I don't remember how I learned to write. My husband came from a family of twelve. We didn't want our children to [have that many brothers

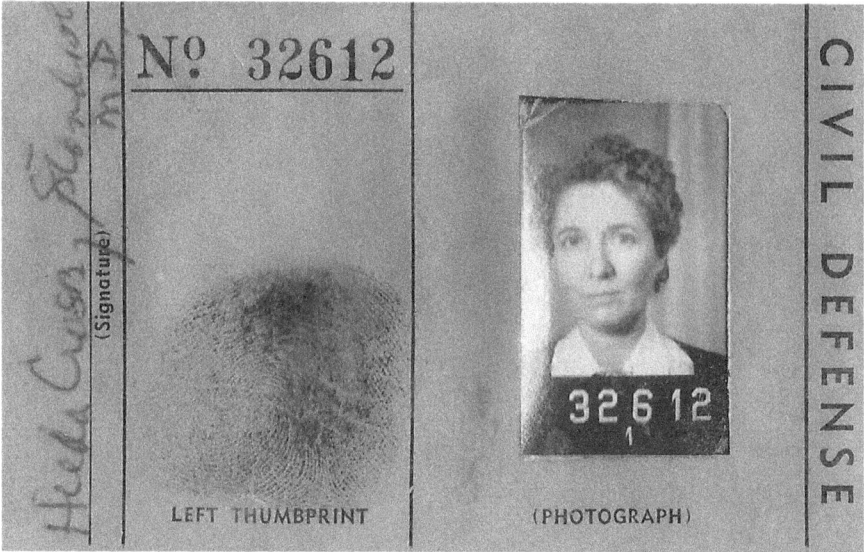

Like many cities, Hartford created a Civil Defense Force in the 1940s in response to the Cold War. Its members were trained to protect and care for civilians if a nuclear bomb or other form of military attack occurred. *Standish family.*

and sisters] *and we wanted a life of our own. I read in the paper that a birth control clinic had opened, so I put my two children in a carriage and pushed them there. With every step I said, 'I am going to Hell. I am going to Hell.' But then I got there, and three kind ladies met me, and I knew it was all right. You were one of those ladies, and you took care of me. And I never told anyone. No one. And we didn't have any more children, and we had a good life, and later we traveled. Now my daughter lives near me, and she phones every day, and I have grandchildren and great-grandchildren. So now you know why I want to throw my arms around you!"*

I invited her to lunch, and we threw our arms around each other.

Still Work to Be Done

Hilda celebrated her 100th birthday by taking a trip to Iceland and Greenland. She died on June 1, 2005, at age 102. Thanks to the Hilda Crosby Standish MD Clinic, her name and legacy still have a visible place in the community. But Judy Tabar is not sure that's enough:

Hilda and her children. *Standish family.*

> *Hilda is a role model we all can use as an inspiration to speak up and advocate for the things we believe in. Her passion and unflappable courage can be applied to any cause. But for those of us who feel strongly about women's health and reproductive rights, we need to remember that the struggle isn't over yet. Hilda's work is, unfortunately, not done. New efforts to block women from reproductive services are popping up all the time, so it's up to us who believe as Hilda did to carry out the cause.*

Hilda would expect no less.

Chapter 11

ELLA GRASSO

GROUNDBREAKING GOVERNOR: 1919–1981

As the first woman in the United States to be elected governor in her own right, Ella Grasso became a national political figure who many saw at the forefront of a new era in politics. As popular nationally as she was at

Ella on the night of her May 1974 gubernatorial primary victory. *Hartford History Center, Hartford Public Library.*

home in Connecticut, her name was often mentioned as a vice presidential nominee or for a U.S. Cabinet or ambassador appointment.

But prestige and power weren't what Ella wanted, said her son Jim Grasso. What she wanted was to be in and help Connecticut. "My mother was really a very simple person who truly loved the state and its people," said Jim, who was in his early twenties when Ella was elected to her first term as governor. "She had no ulterior motives; no desire for wealth or fame. She pushed herself to be the best and do all she could for the Connecticut people, and she was deathly afraid of ever letting them down."

Bright Beginnings, Bright Future

Several firsts can be listed under Ella Grasso's name:
- First woman elected floor leader of the Connecticut General Assembly
- First female chair of the Democratic State Platform Committee
- First Connecticut secretary of state to give the public access to state record and officials whose job it was to answers questions and listen to complaints
- First female governor of Connecticut

The daughter of Italian immigrants, she was also the first U.S. governor of Italian-American descent, as well as the first person in her family to attend and graduate college. Her father, James, was a bakery owner who pretended to know how to read and write, and her mother, Maria, was a millworker who knew how to read but never finished school. The two didn't live to see their daughter become the first woman in the nation to be elected governor without having to run on the record

A young Ella. *Ella T. Grasso Papers, Mount Holyoke College Archives and Special Collections, South Hadley, Massachusetts.*

Ella (center) in a Mount Holyoke College economics class with Professor Everett Hawkins, 1937. *Ella T. Grasso Papers, Mount Holyoke College Archives and Special Collections, South Hadley, Massachusetts.*

of a husband who had also been governor. But perhaps if they did, they wouldn't have been surprised.

Even as a little girl, Ella Giovanna Oliva Tambussi soared to the top. High scores at St. Mary's Elementary School in her hometown of Windsor Locks, Connecticut, earned her a scholarship to attend the nearby but selective private Loomis Chaffee School in Windsor. The yearbook predicted she would be the first woman mayor of Windsor Locks. A scholarship to Mount Holyoke College in Massachusetts in 1936 led to her earning both a bachelor's and master's degree in economics and sociology. Supplementing her scholarship by babysitting and working in a school statistics lab, she graduated magna cum laude and as a Phi Beta Kappa.

Compelled by her school experiences to enter public service, Ella in 1942 took a job as assistant director of research for Connecticut's War Manpower Commission, part of the national agency charged to balance industry and agriculture labor needs during World War II. That same year, she married Hartford teacher and later East Hartford school principal Thomas Grasso, and for three summers, in addition to their other work, they owned and operated a small movie theater called the New Colony in Old Lyme,

One of the only photographs Susane has of herself with her mother. *Susane Grasso.*

Connecticut. Ella ran the box office. Soon after, their daughter, Susane, and son, Jim, were born.

Susane said it was clear to her at an early age that her mother wasn't anything like her friends' mothers:

> *I think it was around eighth grade when it hit me that other kids didn't have mothers who worked 24/7 in the state Capitol. When I think about those days, it's very bittersweet. During the summer, when she was secretary of*

state, I'd go with her to work and hang out in her big office. At lunch we'd go to a restaurant downtown, and everyone who went with us would give me the cherries from their Manhattans. She worked all the time. She was a politician who cared so much about her constituents. She saw every person in the state of Connecticut as a member of her family.

Part of the Solution

Ella's role and significance as a pioneering woman in politics is well documented in letters, newspaper headlines, old TV clips, history books and many other places. Even Ella herself acknowledged the trail she blazed, though she was equally quick to downplay it. "All my friends in the women's movement get angry at me for saying this, but I never thought that being a woman gave me any special political problems," she said during her first term as governor. "It was only when my friends from the foreign press, in New York, kept coming here and writing about me as a woman candidate that I began to think I was doing something unusual."

Her reason for getting involved in politics and public service was a much simpler one, she said: "I realized early on that if I was concerned with problems, the best way of getting them solved was to be part of the decision-making process."

That desire to fix problems and help make decisions led her to spend four years in Connecticut's House of Representatives representing Windsor Locks where, among other accomplishments, she helped rewrite the then 147-year-old state constitution to reflect modern laws and practices and simplify state government by being a driving force for the elimination of county legislators and officials.

Her twelve years as Connecticut secretary of the state—longer than anyone since 1835 had held the position—included leading state efforts to develop the Connecticut Department of Mental Retardation, reorganize the court system and establish more services for the elderly. This, coupled with her reinvention of the secretary of state's office into a "people's lobby," led to a popularity that saw her receiving more votes than the gubernatorial candidates during statewide elections.

It was during this time that with the help and encouragement of Connecticut Democratic State Party leader John Bailey, Ella also began stepping into the national spotlight. In 1968, Bailey made her a delegate to

ELLA T. GRASSO

FOR SECRETARY OF THE STATE

M.H.C. 1940

Ella Tambussi Grasso is a housewife and mother, an educator and an experienced state legislator, well informed on the affairs of Connecticut. She is equipped to understand Connecticut's problems and to act wisely for her state.

The front of a campaign flier. *Ella T. Grasso Papers, Mount Holyoke College Archives and Special Collections, South Hadley, Massachusetts.*

THE WOMAN'S PLACE IS IN THE HOUSE

A profile of Mrs. Ella Grasso — a wife, mother and assistant minority leader in the Legislature

by *Irving M. Kravsow*

A LEGISLATOR'S DAY. At the Grasso home in Windsor Locks it starts when the representative prepares breakfast for her two children, takes Susane to school and leaves James, 4, at his grandmother's. Then it's off to the Capitol where Mrs. Grasso confers with Democratic leaders. In this sequence, she's shown with Gov. Ribicoff discussing items on the day's agenda. Her duties as assistant minority leader in House keep her on the floor and talking much of the day. Late in the afternoon she returns home to prepare dinner for the home arrival of her husband, a school principal and business man.

From the February 20, 1955 *Hartford Courant Magazine*. Ella T. Grasso Papers, Mount Holyoke College Archives and Special Collections, South Hadley, Massachusetts.

the Democratic National Convention, where she pushed for the party's platform to include a plank opposing the Vietnam War and walked out of the Chicago convention hall to protest what she believed was police brutality against antiwar demonstrators.

Two years later, she ran for U.S. Congress from the Sixth District when incumbent Republican Thomas Meskill ran for governor. Republicans won most offices in Connecticut in that election, but Ella was one of the few exceptions. She won and was reelected in 1972. There in Washington, D.C., she served on the House of Representatives' Veterans' Affairs Committee and House Education and Labor Committee. She helped draft the Comprehensive Employment and Training Act, voted for economic-

117

stimulus bills, advocated for liberal social programs and focused huge efforts on turning the economic decline of Bristol, Torrington and other aging industrial cities in her district.

But she found Washington politics, and the House itself, to be unwieldy. It was a slow wheel—much too slow for a woman used to seeing results. And for a woman who grew up and still lived in a tightknit Italian community with her parents across the street and aunts and uncles just a few houses away, weeks passed too slowly. Weekends were spent flying home to her husband and children. Remembered Jim:

> *Mom really was a person shaped by her past, and she loved Windsor Locks and being there with her family. She often said that she got her strength from Windsor Locks, and she maintained connections with people there until she died. Sometimes I think that she could have very easily been first selectman, but that wasn't what she wanted. She wanted to be an advocate for the entire state and its people.*

The "Governess"

Ella in 1970 had successfully replaced Thomas Meskill in the U.S. House, so why not replace him as governor of Connecticut? It was this question that brought Ella back to Connecticut in 1974 to run for the state's top spot rather than for a third term in Congress. It was also an idea Bailey, arguably the most powerful Democrat in the state, supported. But perhaps most importantly, Ella had a firm platform to stand on. Popular and known for being both frugal and against a state income tax, she was known and supported throughout the state.

Despite an ugly campaign that included Republican opponent Robert Steele printing bumper stickers that read "Connecticut Can't Afford a Governess," it was an easy win for Ella. She won with almost 60 percent of the vote, which, among other results, turned the focus of the U.S. television media onto the nation's third-smallest state.

Ella wasn't the first woman in the United States to serve as governor. The first was Carolyn B. Shelton of Oregon, who for three days in 1909 was promoted from chief of staff to acting governor when the state's outgoing governor, George Chamberlain, left for Washington and his new role in the U.S. Senate while incoming governor Frank Benson was ill. Nellie Tayloe

Ella's election as governor put her and Connecticut in the national limelight.

Ross was elected governor of Wyoming in 1924, shortly after her husband, Governor William Ross, died. And that same year, Miriam Ferguson was elected governor of Texas, a position her husband, James, had held seven years earlier.

Ella, however, was the first woman in the United States elected governor without being the wife or widow of a previous governor. It was a distinction that earned her headlines in the *New York Times* and the cover of *Newsweek*.

But it wasn't distinction she was interested in, said current Secretary of State Susan Bysiewicz, whose biography *Ella: A Biography of Ella Grasso* was published in 1984 by the Connecticut Consortium for Law and Citizenship Education. In it, Bysiewicz quotes an October 1974 interview Ella gave to the *Valley Advocate* in which she said, "People aren't looking at me as a woman; they're looking at my stands on major issues. My experience in government has earned me a shot at the office of governor. I've paid my dues. The governorship is neither a man's nor a woman's work. I see it as a people's job."

History books remember how Ella's first term led to important legislation like Connecticut's Freedom of Information Act and the "sunshine" law that opened government functions to public scrutiny. She reorganized the executive branch to make it more efficient and created a strong Department of Public Utilities Control. Residents, however, saw nothing but green.

With Connecticut $70 million in debt left by her predecessor, the green of money—or lack thereof—was first and foremost in both Ella's and the public's eyes. In what many who knew Ella remember as a heart-wrenching time, she broke her campaign promise that she would pass revenue-sharing aid into the municipalities, cut state welfare benefits to below the rate of inflation and, perhaps most memorably, laid off five hundred state workers shortly before Christmas in 1975.

She also laid a deep dividing line when she attempted to extend state employees' workweeks, cut travel by state employees and told them to communicate by postcards rather than letters. Some of these battles ended in compromise, but she lost fights to end legalized gambling and merge the War Veterans Fund into the General Fund.

Known for being a hands-on workaholic who, by her friendliest critics, was called a "tough customer," Ella commonly worked seven days, long into the night and on weekends. To show state workers and residents she wasn't asking anyone for sacrifices she wasn't willing to make herself, she turned in the governor's limousine for a gas-friendly compact car and returned $7,000 of her $42,000 annual salary.

Despite her troubles and dipping popularity, she was reelected in November 1978, arguing that because of the many painful cuts, the state was solvent without the need of an income tax and was experiencing both low unemployment and healthy economic growth. Still, she wasn't without dissenters. Feminists complained that she had appointed too few women to official posts, and old-line politicians accused her of not making appointments in accordance with party lines.

Ella's signature.

Ella's response? "People expect skills. Purely political appointments of persons with no credit other than party affiliations are no longer part of our modern politics."

During this term, her peers elected her chairman of the nationwide Democratic Governors Conference, which she helped convince to throw its support behind President Jimmy Carter for renomination at the 1980 Democratic National Convention, rather than back the favored Massachusetts U.S. senator Edward Kennedy. Carter gained the nod, but Ella was diagnosed with ovarian cancer and unable to continue campaigning.

She Walked a Mile in the Snow

When Ella Grasso died of ovarian cancer on February 5, 1981, in Hartford, then former president Carter, who lost to Republican Ronald Reagan in the general election, issued the following statement:

Ella Grasso represented all that is good and promising about politics and public service. As one of the most prominent women in this country, she had great strength, skill and, when required, toughness. At the same time, she was as loving and compassionate a person as I have known. Her devotion to the less fortunate members of our society was untiring. She faced death with the same courage she faced life.

Courage is a word Susane often associates with her mother. For Jim, those words are "dutiful, loving, compassionate." Those who lived in Connecticut in 1978 tend to match Ella's name with the word "snow."

That winter, thirty hours of storms covered the Nutmeg State in more than two feet of snow that, after all was added up, caused $25 million in damage and forced thousands from along the coast to evacuate their homes. President Carter declared the state a federal disaster area and sent several hundred National Guardsmen to help state Department of Transportation and municipal public works crews shovel and recover. Committed to getting to the State Armory to oversee the crisis, Ella ended up trudging the last mile through knee-high drifts when her car couldn't make it any farther. In an unprecedented move, she ordered the state to shut down for three days, banning drivers from roads and highways while the plows dug out.

In many ways, it was a defining moment for Ella, Susane said: "People who recognize my last name who were here in '78 always have a story to tell about my mother. In some ways, the fondest memories I have of her are those I've heard from other people. It amazes me how to so many people, she is still so beloved."

When Ella's cancer was discovered, several health experts urged her to seek specialized care in New York or Boston. But Ella wouldn't leave Connecticut. As Susane remembered:

> Connecticut was where her heart was, but she left with so many unfinished dreams. When she was dying in Hartford Hospital, the state was finally showing a surplus. But she knew she wasn't going to live to be able to do anything with it. I think that was one of the things she was most disappointed about, though she didn't complain. She believed that even if the cards were stacked against you, you had to fight your way through to the end.

After her death, Ella's body lay in state outside the secretary of state's office at the capitol. Despite heavy rain during the viewing, more than five thousand people from all walks of life trekked to Hartford to pay their respects. At her funeral that was broadcast on radio and TV, Jim Grasso explained why he believed so many people felt her loss so greatly, saying, "She gave to all of you what she gave to my sister, Susane, and me…a mother's gift of unselfish love, understanding, compassion and tenderness."

It was a remarkable goodbye to a remarkable woman who followed the same advice she gave others: "Bloom where you are planted."

Chapter 12

EDYTHE GAINES

FIRST AFRICAN AMERICAN AND FEMALE
SCHOOLS SUPERINTENDENT: 1922–2006

When pioneer educator Edythe Gaines became superintendent of Hartford schools, she also became Connecticut's first female and African American public schools superintendent. A force in the city during the more than thirty years she lived there, she made local headlines in 1978 after making a fiery speech to the Greater Hartford NAACP about the need for African Americans to break out of the political, economic, educational and psychological bondage that she believed was enslaving them in Hartford.

When Edythe died, former Hartford mayor Carrie Saxon Perry—herself remarkable as the first African American woman elected mayor of a large city—remembered Edythe this way, saying, "She was an amazing woman. She was so task-oriented. When she had a project, she was relentless. She had such style and

Edythe at age sixty-five. *Gaines family.*

such class and such drive. She was comfortable moving among everyone. She was a hero in our community."

Always a Teacher

One of seven children of Jacob and Jennie Dillard Jones, Edythe Pauline Jones was born on September 6, 1922, in Asheville, North Carolina, to parents involved in both the community and public life. Her father was an Episcopal priest and her mother a high school English and Latin teacher. And at a young age, it was clear that Edythe was as quick as she was curious. On her first day as a first-grader, she was advanced into the second and then the third grade, which was where she began her education.

As a student at Hunter College. *Gaines family.*

While she was still young, her father died, and the family moved to New York City. There, she met and married Albert Gaines in 1941. She also earned two degrees—a bachelor's from Hunter College and a master's from New York University—and had two sons. Later, she earned a doctorate in education from Harvard University.

Her first teaching position in 1945 was in the New York Public Schools at Joan of Arc School. She quickly earned a reputation as an outspoken and innovative leader, which stayed with her throughout her career. Her son Richard Gaines, a retired lawyer in Pennsylvania, reflected on her ideals as a teacher:

> *She was a person who believed in kids, even when they didn't believe in themselves. Many times, the result was her faith in them would give them faith in themselves. She didn't believe in making lessons easy for kids—in fact, she said making things easy was the worst thing a teacher could do. Learning came from being challenged and being forced to think. She also believed that race and background had nothing to do with a person's capacity to learn or do difficult things. She was adamant that everyone could learn if they put in the effort. There were no excuses for not getting things done, except that you didn't do them.*

In 1964 at Joan of Arc Middle School, where Edythe became the first African American secondary school principal in New York City. *Gaines family.*

At Joan of Arc, Edythe rose quickly through the ranks and, in 1964, became the first African American principal of a New York City school. That same year, she spoke at a United Federation of Teachers panel about "Safeguarding the Concept of Professional in Teaching" in response to what at the time were widespread suggestions that dedicated schools of education might not be the best sources of teacher training. Edythe was ferociously opposed to this idea, challenging that instead of making it easier or more convenient for people to become teachers, it should become more difficult—especially for women entering the field:

> *I may risk my very life in making the next statement, in as much as most of the members of this audience are of the female sex. Still, it must be said that we women, as a group, pose a threat to the concept of professionalism in teaching. Too many women look to teaching as a stopping off place between the end of formal schooling and the beginning of wifehood and motherhood. Such teachers tend not to have a sense of commitment to the profession and this has a depressing effect on the total professionalism of the job. The fact is that the woman who trains as a doctor or as a lawyer is not likely to drop her profession when she marries or has children. Her initial investment has been too great to take so cavalier an attitude. I believe that we must make the professional training of teachers sufficiently rigorous to constitute a similar sense of investment and, therefore, a sense of commitment. There is a corollary to this. Experience has shown that the more rigorous are the requirements for qualification for a profession, the more likely it is that more able people will be attracted to that profession. As long as we keep the training program one in which the lowest third of the college group can easily find success, the more likely it is that the profession will attract the lowest third and that it will be unattractive to the most able students.*

In 1967, she became assistant superintendent of School District 12 in the Bronx and, in 1973, was named executive director of the New York City Board of Education's Office of Educational Planning and Support, one of three senior administrative posts just a step below the citywide chancellor.

In 1975, Edythe's career moves, reputation and deep commitment to youth education initiatives led to her being offered the position of Hartford's first African American superintendent of schools. The appointment also made her the first woman in Connecticut to hold the post. National attention for the achievement followed, including *Ebony* magazine featuring Edythe as one of several dozen African American public officials across the country whose salary was conspicuously lower than their white counterparts. But unfortunately, Edythe's tenure was short-lived, ending in 1978 over politics and what the editors of New London's the *Day* called "a loss for all." Much of their editorial about this "extraordinary woman...[who] is black" is worth sharing:

> *When she was appointed, great things were expected by Mrs. Gaines, by the school board. Hartford has 28,000 pupils in its public schools. Fifty percent are black and another one-third are Spanish speaking...Clearly, Hartford needed—still needs—a leader capable of making a school system work to the advantage of children, to the advantage of the city.*
>
> *Her greatest support came from the then-president of the school board, Scott McAlister, a tough-minded, forward-looking intelligent insurance executive. McAlister died of lung cancer soon thereafter. Had he lived...*
>
> *School board direction passed to one of those bland coalitions in which a racially-mixed public board gets along together, just barely. Friction developed between the board and Mrs. Gaines. Somewhere along the line, Mrs. Gaines' unique talent and imagination, together with the original goals, lost priority. Increasingly, she applied her techniques and ideas without consulting the board. In the end, the establishment acted by not renewing her contract.*
>
> *This is a tragedy for Hartford and its children. To this day, few doubt that Edythe Gaines has the right answers for the special needs of Hartford and other urban centers...Edythe Gaines went far out, well beyond the constrictions of time-honored and inflexible structures of procedure. She is typical of many talented black Americans. They easily recognize problems their white brethren have had no opportunity to consider because of racial insulation. They not only have defined those problems but have effective solutions.*

This extraordinary editorial did much to show the damage that fear and discrimination can incur. Yet despite her critics and a very public disappointment in the Hartford board's decision, Edythe remained committed to the community, choosing to stay in Hartford and continuing to play an important leadership role in education, healthcare and the arts.

Even in the face of hurt or disappointment, she had a strong sense of her self-worth and abilities, which helped her overcome any challenge, said her son Mallory Gaines of New Jersey. A true public servant, she served as an

Edythe's signature.

active board member of several Hartford nonprofits, including the Urban League, United Way, Hartford Stage, Connecticut Opera, The Bushnell, Connecticut Public Broadcasting, United Health Appeal, Hartford Hospital, Mount Sinai Hospital and the Institute of Living and Newington Children's Hospital. Inspired by Edythe, Mallory taught elementary and high school for twenty-five years, and he said, "She had a sense of humor that helped her get through any situation, but most importantly an extremely keen mind that allowed her to reason, recognize the details of a situation, and then make a decision. She also said that belief in yourself was everlasting. No one could take that away. She passed that belief on to me, and I tried to pass it on to my students."

A Statewide Role

From 1979 to 1991, Edythe served as a commissioner for the State Department of Public Utility Control. In 1992, she was named to the Board of Governors of Higher Education, and in 1995, she was given the opportunity to serve a four-year term on the Connecticut State Board of Education. She was the only African American on the nine-member panel responsible for setting education policy for public schools across the state. It was a most appropriate appointment. Her race gave the board much-needed diversity, and her passion to inspire students' success was often seen as contagious. When she spoke, it was with power and conviction, as illustrated when she spoke before the United Federation of Teachers about what constitutes a successful teacher:

What do I mean by "the professional teacher?" First, he is a teacher who is skilled in his craft, nay art, and who day by day, week by week, year by year consistently seeks to improve upon present performance. He doesn't need to be told to plan his work; he knows that this is foundational to his growth. He doesn't need to be told to attend professional conferences and conventions or to observe other teachers or to read the professional literature. He knows that he will gain by participating in the market place of fresh and useful ideas. He doesn't need to be told to join and participate in organizations and programs whose purpose is the advancement of the whole profession. He knows that his welfare is inextricably bound to the welfare of others in his profession...

The professional teacher knows down deep "where he lives" that all of the children are his children. He knows that his work goes beyond the four walls of his classroom, beyond the community to which he is specifically assigned, beyond the confines of the academic subject matter he has been "prepared" to teach. He knows that he is a teacher of all children, a guardian of our nation's most precious possession, wherever they may be and whatever their present status.

When she submitted her resignation after just two years, Board President Allan B. Taylor lamented how difficult Edythe would be to replace when he said, "Everybody on the board will miss her greatly. She had an unwavering insistence that we maintain a set of high expectations for all our students. "

Edythe backed up her beliefs about the importance of public service by being an active volunteer, especially in the area of Hartford near her home on the corner of Kenyon and Asylum Streets. There, she served as the chair of the Commission on Ministry of the Episcopal Diocese of Connecticut and represented St. Monica's Episcopal Church as chairwoman. She spearheaded St. Monica's Development Corporation's Second Century Project, a multimillion dollar effort that built houses for the elderly while also providing numerous health and human service initiatives. In 1991, she was honored by the National Association of Negro Business and Professional Women's Clubs for her work to establish affordable housing for the elderly. Gaines was also the first woman to be

An official portrait. *Gaines family.*

elected chair of a Harvard University alumni association and has been inducted into the Hunter College Hall of Fame.

However, wherever she was or whatever she was doing, Edythe was a teacher first, said her grandson Cory Gaines of California, who was forty-one when she died:

On holidays, we'd have massive debates about whatever was the contemporary topic of the day, and sometimes the conversations got heated. But that was OK, because my Grandmother Gaines loved debate. She loved expressing ideas and really, in every way, represented success to me. We'd get dressed up to go to her house, and it made sense because every time we got together, she made it feel like a celebration. She was successful, and she believed that all of us grandkids could be successful too. My father and uncle told me that she was the type of person I wanted to aspire to be. She represented the best in our family, and the best of black culture in general, because she was the epitome of success. She had an advanced education, she was articulate in thought and reason, she cared deeply about other people, and I'd see when we were out around Hartford that she had earned the respect of those in both the black and white communities.

Not Ordinary, Extraordinary

Edythe Gaines died in Hartford on March 23, 2006, at the age of eighty-three. A dozen years before, Connecticut Historical Society officials asked her to write the introduction for their book *Black Women of Connecticut: Achievements Against the Odds*. Edythe offered the following thoughts on the women readers would meet within its pages:

With husband, Albert, and sons, Richard and Mallory, in 1982, celebrating Edythe and Albert's fortieth wedding anniversary. *Gaines family.*

Ultimately, you will come to realize that these "ordinary" women have been extraordinarily instrumental in your own life, usually unbeknownst to you, since they have been instrumental in shaping the quality of life of the people of Connecticut and of those beyond its borders—black and white, male and female…Make your own discoveries as you probe deeper and deeper into that which is offered to you in the pages of this book, and into the wider research you should be led to pursue after tasting what is provided here.

Draw near. Read of these extraordinary women. Learn from them. Learn from their heritage of excellence.

The same should be said about Edythe.

TIMELINE

REMARKABLE EVENTS IN HARTFORD
WOMEN'S HISTORY

Note: Names of the women featured in this book are highlighted in bold.

Hartford's beginnings coincide with the United States' beginnings. Two years after traders from the Dutch West India Company built a trading house called Fort Hoop on what's now known as Hartford's Park River, English settlers arrived in 1635 and established a village. In 1637, that village was named Hartford. As the young country grew, so—though too slowly—did public documentation and recognition of the accomplishments achieved by the women who lived and worked there. Among those most notable:

1777: **Hannah Bunce Watson** takes the helm of the *Connecticut Courant* and becomes one of the first female newspaper publishers in the United States. To date, only two women have served as publishers of what is now the *Hartford Courant:* Hannah and Marty Petty.

1815: **Lydia Huntley Sigourney** publishes her first book, *Moral Pieces in Prose and Verse.* Over the next several years, her productivity and popularity lead to her becoming one of the first self-supporting female writers in America.

1823: Harford Female Seminary is founded by Catharine Beecher and becomes one of the first major educational institutions for women in the United States. **Harriet Beecher Stowe** and **Virginia Thrall Smith** are among those who attend.

1851: The first installment of **Harriet Beecher Stowe**'s *Uncle Tom's Cabin* appears in the *National Era*.

1860: Isabella Beecher Hooker, **Harriet Beecher Stowe**'s sister, founds the Connecticut Woman Suffrage Association.

1862: **Elizabeth Colt** takes over as head of Colt Manufacturing after her husband, Samuel, dies and guides the business through its greatest period of prosperity.

1869: **Elizabeth Colt** helps organize the first Connecticut Suffragette Convention.

1881: **Virginia Thrall Smith** establishes the first free kindergarten in Connecticut at the Hartford City Missionary Society.

1898: Hartford resident Charlotte Perkins Gilman writes the groundbreaking *Women in Economics*. In the years that follow, her short story "The Yellow Wallpaper" is recognized as one of the first pieces of feminist fiction.

1905: Per instructions left in her will, **Elizabeth Colt**'s philanthropy leads to the creation of a new wing at Hartford's Wadsworth Atheneum. Several years earlier, she established the first public art and picture gallery in the United States.

1913: Katherine Houghton Hepburn organizes the Hartford Equal Franchise League, which evolves into the Connecticut Woman's Suffrage Association.

1917: **Mary Townsend Seymour** co-founds the Greater Hartford chapter of the NAACP.

1918: Suffragists rally in Hartford and Simsbury, asking President Woodrow Wilson for help in getting women the right to vote.

1920: The same year the Nineteenth Amendment is ratified to give women the right to vote, **Mary Townsend Seymour** becomes the first African American woman in the United States to run for a state office. She also goes undercover to help African American women working in Connecticut tobacco fields organize against unfair labor practices.

1923: The Connecticut Birth Control League is founded. Four decades later, it becomes Planned Parenthood.

1930: The Horace Bushnell Memorial Hall opens, thanks to **Dotha Bushnell Hillyer**'s commitment not just to keeping her father's memory alive but also to making a difference in Hartford.

1932: Shortly before her death, **Dotha Bushnell Hillyer** and her husband establish Hillyer Junior College, which in 1957 becomes part of the University of Hartford.

1933: **Rachel Taylor Milton** co-founds the Urban League of Hartford. Also this year, Hartford College for Women opens as part of the University of Hartford.

1935: **Hilda Crosby Standish** becomes medical director of Connecticut's first birth control clinic in Hartford and establishes herself as a pioneer in sex education and family planning.

1938: **Beatrice Fox Auerbach** becomes president of G. Fox, a position she'll hold for twenty-seven years, innovating workplace and labor practices that are adapted by businesses throughout the United States.

1945: **Beatrice Fox Auerbach** founds the Service Bureau for Women's Organizations.

1961: To challenge Connecticut's birth control ban, Estelle Griswold of Hartford opens a birth control clinic in New Haven and is arrested for dispensing contraceptives. Her arrest leads to the 1965 Supreme Court decision *Griswold v. Connecticut*, which makes birth control legal and declares it unconstitutional for a government to control a woman's reproductive health decisions.

1968: **Harriet Beecher Stowe** house on Forest Street becomes a museum and opens to the public.

1987: Carrie Saxon Perry is elected mayor of Hartford, becoming the first African American woman to head a New England City.

1973: The Permanent Commission on the Status of Women and Connecticut Women's Education and Legal Fund are established.

1974: **Ella Grasso** is elected the first female governor of Connecticut, as well as the first female governor in the United States elected in her own right. She is also the nation's first Italian-American governor.

1975: **Edythe Gaines** becomes superintendent of Hartford public schools—the first woman and first African American to lead a Connecticut school system.

1980: Connecticut's Unfair Employment Practices Act makes sexual harassment illegal, and President Jimmy Carter declares March to be National Women's History Month.

1988: Hartford resident and Puerto Rican native Maria Sanchez becomes the first Latino woman elected to the Connecticut General Assembly.

1990: Eunice Groark is elected the first female lieutenant governor in Connecticut.

1991: U.S. congresswoman Barbara Kennelly of Hartford becomes the first woman to serve as deputy majority whip of the U.S. House of Representatives and on the House Intelligence Committee.

1993: The Connecticut Women's Hall of Fame is founded and holds its first induction ceremony in Hartford.

1994: Nancy Wyman becomes the first woman to be elected Connecticut comptroller.

1998: Denise Napier of Hartford becomes the first woman and first African American elected Connecticut treasurer.

2004: Connecticut's second woman governor, Jodi Rell, is sworn in at the capitol. She holds the position until 2011, after she decides not to run for a third term.

2010: For the first time in Connecticut legislative history, two African American women chair the powerful Appropriations Committee, Senators Toni Harp and Toni Walker.

BIBLIOGRAPHY

Anderson, Patricia. Untitled report. Yale Divinity School, 1986.

Benton, Byron, and Kelly Gineo. "Hannah Bunce Watson Hudson in Old South Burying Ground, Hartford CT: Woman Publisher and Patriot." *People of Old South Burying Ground,* Connecticut Gravestone Network. Last modified 2012. http://www.ctgravestones.com/CTprojects/old_south.htm.

The Bushnell. Last modified 2013. http://bushnell.org.

Bysiewicz, Susan. *Ella: A Biography of Governor Ella Grasso.* Hartford: Connecticut Consortium for Law and Citizenship Education, Inc., 1984.

Campbell, Susan. "Beatrice Fox Auerbach Used Wealth to Care." *Hartford Courant,* January 1, 2012. http://courant.com.

Cohen, Linda Smith. "A Social Visionary Left a Message That's Still Timely." *Hartford Courant,* November 5, 1995.

———. "Virginia Thrall Smith: Hartford City Missionary and Social Reformer." MA diss., Trinity College, 1990.

Collin, Grace Lathrop. "Lydia Huntley Sigourney." *New England Magazine: An Illustrated Monthly* 27, 1902.

Connecticut Historical Society. Last modified 2013. http://www.connecticuthistory.org.

Connecticut Women's Hall of Fame. Last modified 2013. http://www.cwhf.org.

Coote, Albert W. *Four Vintage Decades: The Performing Arts in Hartford.* Hartford: Huntington, 1970.

"Death of Mrs. Stowe." *Hartford Courant,* July 2, 1896. ProQuest Historical Newspapers: Hartford Courant (1764–1922). http://nhregister.com.

"Essex Books Co-hosts Author Dr. Virginia Hale." *Valley News,* December 1, 2010.

Fenster, Jordan. "She Was Known as Ella: Biography of Connecticut's First Female Governor Details Character, Charisma." *New Haven Register,* March 24, 2012.

Fox, Margalit. "Edythe Gaines, 83, a Top-Ranked Educator, Dies." *New York Times,* April 1, 2006. http://nytimes.com.

Gaines, Edythe J. Introduction to *Black Women of Connecticut, Achievement Against the Odds.* N.p.: Connecticut Historical Society, 1984.

———. "Safeguarding the Concept of Professionalism in Teaching." *Hunter Alumni Quarterly* (January 1964).

Garrow, David J. "The Legal Legacy of *Griswold v. Connecticut.*" *Human Rights* 38, no. 2 (Spring 2011): 26–25. *Academic Search Premier,* EBSCOhost (accessed December 20, 2013).

Gottlieb, Rachel. "A Life of Inspiration in City Ends." *Hartford Courant,* March 24, 2006. http://courant.com.

"Harriet Beecher Stowe: Death of the Authoress of 'Uncle Tom's Cabin.'" *New York Times,* July 2, 1896. http://nytimes.com.

"Hartford's Loss a Loss for All of Us." *Day,* May 17, 1978.

Henry, Susan. "Work, Widowhood and War: Hannah Bunce Watson, Connecticut Printer." *Connecticut Historical Society Bulletin* (Winter 1983): 25–39.

"Highest-Paid Black Public Officials." *Ebony* 33, no. 5 (March 1978): 25. *MasterFILE Premier,* EBSCOhost (accessed December 20, 2013).

Hoadly, Charles J. *The Public Records of the State of Connecticut, October 1776–February 1778 inclusive.* Hartford: Case, Lockwood & Brainard Company, 1894.

Jones, Mark H. "Audacious Alliances." *Hog River Journal* 1, no. 4 (Fall 2002).

———. "'To Tell Our Story': Mary Townsend Seymour and the Early Years of Hartford's Branch of the National Association for the Advancement of Colored People, 1917–1920." *Connecticut History* 44, no. 2 (Fall 2005): 205.

Mackenzie, William Douglas. "Dotha Bushnell Hillyer." *Promoter* (January 1933).

"Merited Tribute to a Cultured Woman." *Hartford Courant,* September 11, 1952. ProQuest Historical Newspapers: Hartford Courant (1923–1984).

Miller, Robert. "Remembering Ella, 30 Years Later." *Danbury News-Times*, February 4, 2012. http://www.newstimes.com.

Milton, Rachel Taylor. Letter to the editor. *Hartford Courant*, September 24, 1969.

"Milton, Rachel (Taylor)" in Obituaries. *Hartford Courant*, July 8, 1995. http://courant.com.

Mount Holyoke Archives and Special Collections: Ella T. Grasso Papers: An Online Exhibit, last modified 2013. http://www.mtholyoke.edu.

"Mrs. Beatrice Fox Auerbach, 81, Retailer and Philanthropist, Dies." *New York Times*, December 1, 1968. http://nytimes.com.

"Mrs. Colt Dies of Paralysis." *Hartford Courant*, August 24, 1905. ProQuest Historical Newspapers: Hartford Courant (1764–1922).

"Mrs. Colt's Funeral." *Hartford Courant*, August 25, 1905. ProQuest Historical Newspapers: Hartford Courant (1764–1922).

"Mrs. Mary T. Seymour, NAACP Leader, Dies." *Hartford Courant*, January 14, 1957. ProQuest Historical Newspapers: Hartford Courant (1923–1984).

"Mrs. Virginia Smith: Death of a Former City Missionary and Almoner." *Hartford Courant*, January 5, 1903. ProQuest Historical Newspapers: Hartford Courant (1764–1922).

MucNulty, John Bard. *Older Than the Nation: The Story of the Hartford Courant*. Guilford: Pequot Press, 1964.

Planned Parenthood. "About Us." Last modified 2013. http://plannedparenthood.org.

"Property Conveyed to Bushnell Corp." *Hartford Courant*, July 23, 1920. ProQuest Historical Newspapers: Hartford Courant (1764–1922).

Reisman, Lisa. "Thoroughly Modern: The Story of Beatrice Fox Auerbach." *Shoreline Times*, January 13, 2011. http://www.shorelinetimes.com.

Seymour, Mary Townsend. Letter to the editor. *Hartford Courant*, July 2, 1918. ProQuest Historical Newspapers: Hartford Courant (1923–1984).

Sigourney, Lydia Howard Huntley. *Letters of Life*. 1867. E-text at the Internet Archive. http://archive.org.

Smith, Virginia Thrall. "The Kindergarten" in *The Eagle*, a publication of the Congress of Women, World's Columbian Exposition, ed. Mary Kavanaugh. Chicago, 1893.

Thody, Ron. "Molder of Human Dignity." *Hartford Times Sunday Magazine*, February 1, 1970, 3–4.

"Two Homes in Which Mrs. Sigourney Lived." *Hartford Courant*, November 28, 1906. ProQuest Historical Newspapers: Hartford Courant (1764–1922).

"Virginia Thrall Smith (1836–1903)." Cedar Hill Cemetery Foundation. Last modified 2013. http://www.cedarhillfoundation.org.

Wald, Matthew. "Ex-Gov. Grasso of Connecticut Dead of Cancer." *New York Times*, February 6, 1981. http://nytimes.com.

Wellesley College Alumnae Association. Last modified 2013. http://web.wellesley.edu.

Wheeler, Sandra. "Beatrice Fox Auerbach: 1887–1968." *Jewish Women: A Comprehensive Historical Encyclopedia*. March 1, 2009. Jewish Women's Archive. http://jwa.org/encyclopedia.

INDEX

ABOUT THE AUTHOR

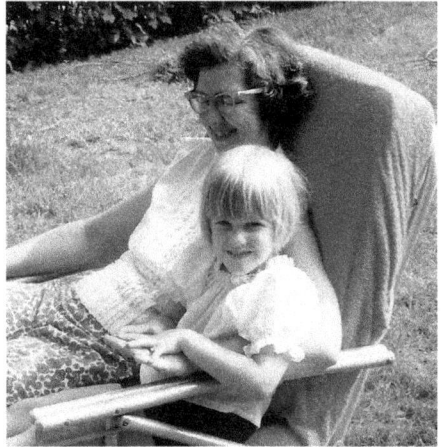

This 1970s photograph shows author Cynthia Wolfe Boynton with another remarkable woman: her mother, Barbara Wolfe, who since 1998 has struggled with advanced Parkinson's disease and—like the women in this book did—faces each day with courage, purpose and love.

An award-winning journalist, playwright and poet, Cindy is a freelance writer whose background includes more than fifteen years as a regular correspondent for the *New York Times* and nine years as editor and publishing director of *Better Health* magazine. Her two most recent plays, *Right Time to Say I Love You* and *Dear Prudence*, both made their premieres in New York City, just steps off Broadway, at the 2011 and 2013 United Solo Theatre Festival. *Right Time* continued with performances that took her to Brighton, England, and one of the largest theater festivals in the world.

A Connecticut resident, Cindy is also an English and communications instructor at the Yale School of Medicine and Housatonic Community College, as well as host of the weekly Literary New England Radio Show podcast. Her proudest accomplishments, however, are her sons, Teddy and Steven.

Fascinated by history and drawn to telling stories about strong women like those included in *Remarkable Women of Hartford*, her website is www. cindywolfeboynton.com.